my **revision** notes

WJEC GCSE

ICT

2ND EDITION

Ian Paget

HODDER
EDUCATION
AN HACHETTE UK COMPANY

The Publishers would like to thank the following for permission to reproduce copyright material.

Photo credits

Page 8 © Keith Morris/Alamy Stock Photo; page 9 © Stewart Cook/Rex/Shutterstock; page 10 © Haris Rauf – Fotolia; page 12 © Sascha Burkard – Fotolia; page 29 © Sheila Paget; page 51 © Hugh Threlfall/Alamy Stock Photo; page 68 © Urbanmyth/Alamy Stock Photo; page 69 © Ian Paget; page 77 © Anthony Maragou – Fotolia; page 82 © Micha Theiner/Rex/Shutterstock. Google and the Google logo are registered trademarks of Google Inc., used with permission.

Every effort has been made to trace all copyright holders, but if any have been inadvertently overlooked, the Publishers will be pleased to make the necessary arrangements at the first opportunity.

Although every effort has been made to ensure that website addresses are correct at time of going to press, Hodder Education cannot be held responsible for the content of any website mentioned in this book. It is sometimes possible to find a relocated web page by typing in the address of the home page for a website in the URL window of your browser.

Hachette UK's policy is to use papers that are natural, renewable and recyclable products and made from wood grown in sustainable forests. The logging and manufacturing processes are expected to conform to the environmental regulations of the country of origin.

Orders: please contact Bookpoint Ltd, 130 Park Drive, Milton Park, Abingdon, Oxon OX14 4SE. Telephone: +44 (0)1235 827827. Fax: +44 (0)1235 400401. Email education@bookpoint.co.uk Lines are open from 9 a.m. to 5 p.m., Monday to Saturday, with a 24-hour message answering service. You can also order through our website: www.hoddereducation.co.uk

ISBN: 978 1 510 45494 1

Cover photo © 3desc – stock.adobe.com
Illustrations by Mike Parsons, Barking Dog Art
Typeset in the United Kingdom and India
Printed in India

A catalogue record for this title is available from the British Library.

Get the most from this book

This book will help you revise units 1 and 3 of the new WJEC ICT GCSE specification. You can use the contents list on pages 2 and 3 to plan your revision, topic by topic. Tick each box when you have:

1 revised and understood a topic

2 tested yourself

3 checked your answers online

You can also keep track of your revision by ticking off each topic heading through the book. You may find it helpful to add your own notes as you work through each topic.

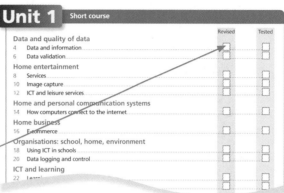

 Tick to track your progress

Exam tip

Throughout the book there are exam tips that explain how you can boost your final grade.

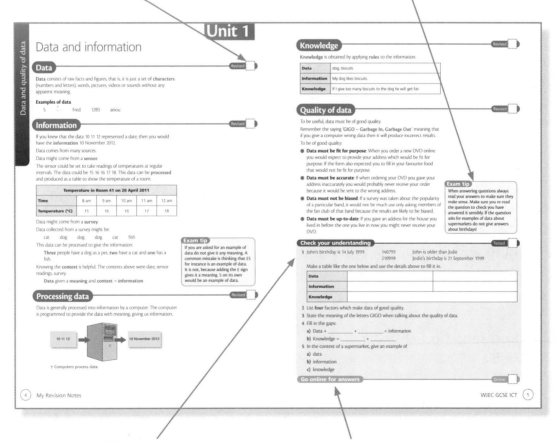

Check your understanding

Use these questions at the end of each section to make sure that you have understood every topic.

Go online

Go online to check your answers at www.hoddereducation.co.uk/myrevisionnotes

Contents and revision planner

Unit 1 — Short course

Unit 3   Full course

Answers to Check your understanding are online:
www.hoddereducation.co.uk/myrevisionnotes

Data and information

Data

Data consists of raw facts and figures, that is, it is just a set of **characters** (numbers and letters), words, pictures, videos or sounds without any apparent meaning.

Examples of data

5   Fred   12B3   aeiou

Information

If you knew that the data 10 11 12 represented a date, then you would have the **information** 10 November 2012.

Data comes from many sources.

Data might come from a **sensor**.

The sensor could be set to take readings of temperatures at regular intervals. The data could be 15 16 16 17 18. This data can be **processed** and produced as a table to show the temperature of a room.

Temperature in Room 41 on 20 April 2011					
Time	8 am	9 am	10 am	11 am	12 am
Temperature (°C)	15	16	16	17	18

Data might come from a **survey**.

Data collected from a survey might be:

cat   dog   dog   dog   cat   fish

This data can be processed to give the information:

Three people have a dog as a pet, **two** have a cat and **one** has a fish.

Knowing the **context** is helpful. The contexts above were date, sensor readings, survey.

Data given a **meaning** and **context** = **information**

> **Exam tip**
>
> If you are asked for an example of data do not give it any meaning. A common mistake is thinking that £5 for instance is an example of data. It is not, because adding the £ sign gives it a meaning. 5 on its own would be an example of data.

Processing data

Data is generally processed into information by a computer. The computer is programmed to provide the data with meaning, giving us information.

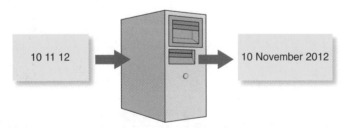

↑ **Computers process data**

Knowledge is obtained by applying **rules** to the information.

Data	dog, biscuits
Information	My dog likes biscuits.
Knowledge	If I give too many biscuits to the dog he will get fat.

Quality of data
Revised

To be useful, data must be of good quality.

Remember the saying '**GIGO – Garbage In, Garbage Out**' meaning that if you give a computer wrong data then it will produce incorrect results.

To be of good quality:

- **Data must be fit for purpose**: When you order a new DVD online you would expect to provide your address which would be fit for purpose. If the form also expected you to fill in your favourite food that would not be fit for purpose.

- **Data must be accurate**: If when ordering your DVD you gave your address inaccurately you would probably never receive your order because it would be sent to the wrong address.

- **Data must not be biased**: If a survey was taken about the popularity of a particular band, it would not be much use only asking members of the fan club of that band because the results are likely to be biased.

- **Data must be up to date**: If you gave an address for the house you lived in before the one you live in now you might never receive your DVD.

Exam tip

When answering questions always read your answers to make sure they make sense. Make sure you re-read the question to check you have answered it sensibly. If the question asks for examples of data about supermarkets do not give answers about birthdays!

Check your understanding
Tested

1 John's birthday is 14 July 1999   140799   John is older than Jodie
                                          210999   Jodie's birthday is 21 September 1999

Make a table like the one below and use the details above to fill it in.

Data		
Information		
Knowledge		

2 List **four** factors which make data of good quality.

3 State the meaning of the letters GIGO when talking about the quality of data.

4 Fill in the gaps:

  a) Data + _____ + _____ = information

  b) Knowledge = _____ + _____

5 In the context of a supermarket, give an example of

  a) data

  b) information

  c) knowledge

Go online for answers
Online

Data validation

Errors

Errors can easily happen to data. Data could be

- collected and recorded wrongly
- entered into the computer incorrectly
- processed incorrectly
- deliberately or accidentally changed by unauthorised people (hacking)
- become corrupted when being transmitted from one computer to another.

Remember GIGO? – If errors can occur when handling data, then we must make sure that the data we are using is as error-free as possible.

↑ **Garbage in, Garbage out**

Exam tip

Do **not** make the mistake in the exam of writing that the data must be checked to see if it is correct. To check that the data is correct would be almost impossible. We can check that it is sensible or that it has been copied correctly, but we have no way of knowing if it was correct to start with. Learn the definitions given on these pages.

Possible sources of errors and the cure

Problem: Data is often collected from forms filled in by people, such as customers filling in forms in the newspaper. These are called **data capture forms**. The person who fills in the form may make a mistake and write down the wrong data.

Cure: Make sure that the forms are designed carefully such as using boxes to fill in or drop-down lists on online forms to limit the possible user choices. Instructions should be clear.

↑ **Validation can check for errors in input**

Problem: Data from the forms has to be copied into the computer. This can lead to copying errors known as **transcription errors**.

Cure: Data **verification** checks for transcription errors. Verification can be done by a human who carefully checks over the original data and makes sure that it is copied correctly, or by the computer. (There is more about verification on page 7).

Problem: The data is not sensible or **valid**. For instance someone puts their date of birth in a form as 30 February 1998 or someone orders 1.5 pairs of shoes.

Cure: **Data validation** is used to check that data is sensible before it is processed. There are quite a few different validation methods and they all have names. Some of these methods are shown below.

- **Range check:** Numerical data is checked to see if the value lies within an acceptable range of numbers. The computer is given a range between which the data must lie for it to be sensible. For instance you would expect a man's height to be somewhere between 1 m and 2.5 m. This is the **range** of heights we might sensibly expect.

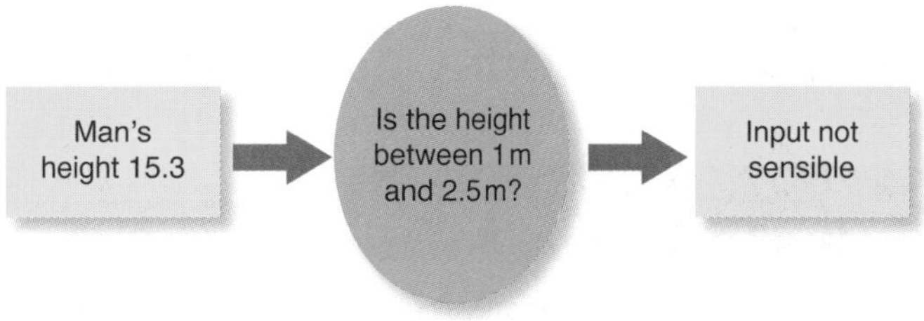

↑ **Range check**

- **Presence check:** Sometimes it is essential to have an item of **data present**. For example, if you are ordering a pair of shoes online, then it is essential that you put in the size you want. If that data is missing, then an error message will appear. You may not be able to fill in any more of the form until that field is completed.
- **Format check:** Some data has to be laid out in an agreed way. A format check will look at the data to see if it conforms to the rules for that data item. For example, a postcode (GL19 3ZZ). Getting the order wrong would cause an error.
- **Check digit:** It is easy to type in digits in the wrong order. For example, when you are typing in a barcode or an ISBN number. This is known as making a **transposition error**. A check digit carries out a calculation on the digits of the number to create an extra digit that is then placed onto the end of the number. When the number is entered, the computer checks the calculation to see if the check digit matches.
- **Lookup check:** Takes the value that has been entered and compares it against a list of values in a table. If the value is not in that list, then an error message is produced.

Exam tip

Remember we can never stop errors of data completely. We can only minimise them with checks such as **verification** and **validation**.

Check your understanding

Tested

1 List **four** possible causes of error that could make data useless.

2 For each of the following, say which type of validation check could have prevented the error.

Data entered	Correct data	Type of validation check
GLL93 5ZZ	GL93 5ZZ	
23.2	2.32	
9 781906 71106 0	9 781906 71106 1	

3 This sentence contains a **transition error**.

Remove the saucepan form the stove before adding the spices.

a) Write down the word that is wrong. What should it have been?

b) What type of check could be used to spot this kind of error?

4 **a)** Explain why the following online data would **not** be acceptable.

Monster Shirt Sale					
Size	Medium	**Colour**		**Type**	T-shirt

b) What kind of validation check would be used to spot this error?

5 Write down a suitable range check for checking examination scores. (The examination is out of 75.)

Go online for answers

Online

Home entertainment

Pay-per-view services

Revised

Pay-per-view (**PPV**) television services are generally associated with **cable** and **satellite** television services. You pay a subscription and then you pay an agreed amount for each film or live sporting event you watch. You can choose what you want to watch, rather than using the standard programmes offered by the TV companies. Pay-per-view services will also let you see other services such as Freeview.

Interactive services

Revised

An **interactive** system is one in which the user is able to make requests to the system and the system is able to react to those requests.

Some interactive services are

- betting, where you are able to place bets on events while you are watching the TV
- dating, which is looking for partners by seeing pictures or profiles on the TV and responding using a remote control
- gaming
- shopping
- voting, which is often connected to game shows and talent competitions, but one day may be used for voting for laws or politicians.

Interactive services	
Advantages	**Disadvantages**
<ul><li>The user is being active rather than passive.</li><li>A number of different activities can be carried out on one system.</li><li>The pictures are often of better quality.</li><li>There is often a choice of language.</li><li>There are possibilities for interactive learning.</li></ul>	<ul><li>There might be arguments over which vote to cast or which camera angle to look at.</li><li>It could lead to becoming a 'couch potato'.</li><li>It can be expensive.</li></ul>

Exam tip

Be careful with your spelling in an examination. For example, there are **programmes** on TV, but the instructions that run on a computer, such as for games, are known as **programs**.

Online services

Revised

All the services above are available using a computer connected to the internet. Some services are extremely popular, such as eBay® trading and shopping with companies like Amazon.

Gaming

Revised

One very popular service is **online gaming**. Here you are able to join in games with people all over the world. Some games are vast with millions of players. You often adopt a **persona** which means you can enter the game as an imaginary character rather than as yourself. Some games are free and others can be joined after you have paid a subscription.

Games consoles

Revised

These are specialist devices for playing games. They often allow you to link to the television screen. **Gamepads** have special controls to help you play games. Some allow you to move about and simulate playing games such as tennis.

Using computers for playing games	
Advantages	**Disadvantages**
● Some games can be educational. ● Games can also be simulations where real-life situations (e.g. learning to fly) can be practised. ● Many games are collaborative and involve team work. ● Some games require quick thinking and good hand–eye coordination might be developed. ● Games that normally need more than one player, such as chess, can be played alone.	● Research indicates that computer games are a form of addiction. ● Playing games alone might limit the development of social skills. ● Gamers may not get enough exercise.

Input and output

Revised

Input devices are needed for data to be input to the system. **Output devices** allow data out of the system.

Virtual reality	Gaming
Input ● Mouse ● Keyboard ● Special gloves **Output** ● Screen ● Headset ● Speakers	**Input** ● Keyboard ● Gamepad ● Joystick ● Mouse **Output** ● Monitor or screen ● Speakers

Exam tip

When answering questions in an ICT examination use the technical terms you have learnt. For example, words like **input** and **output** are technical terms in ICT. The programs that give the computer its instructions are known as **software**. The devices which make up a computer system are known as **hardware**.

Check your understanding

Tested

1 Name **four** services you might find on interactive TV.

2 For each of the following, tick the appropriate box to show whether it is an input or output device.

Device	Input	Output
Computer monitor		
Speaker		
Mouse		
Joystick		

3 Use **one** sentence to describe Pay-per-view TV.

4 Give **two** advantages and **one** disadvantage of playing computer games.

Go online for answers

Online

Image capture

Digital photography

Digital photography is a way of capturing an image without the use of film. The images captured are in electronic format so they can easily be

- transmitted over the internet and published on websites
- displayed in electronic picture frames or albums
- placed on websites for relatives or friends to be able to access from anywhere in the world
- manipulated using specialist software
- printed out using a colour printer
- saved on magnetic or optical media
- sent to someone using a mobile phone.

You can often shoot short movies with digital cameras. These videos can also be downloaded and stored on disk or published on a website.

Exam tip

The word **digital** in ICT terms means using 0s and 1s for storing or communicating data. So a **digital image** is one stored in the computer as millions of 0s and 1s. Use of technical language, such as 'digital', helps to show the examiner that you understand ICT.

Digital camera

Images are stored in a digital camera as digital files on a **flash memory card**. Many computers have flash memory interfaces so that the memory card can be removed from the camera and the images downloaded directly into a computer and saved on backing stores such as hard disk, DVD or CD.

Blu-ray® recorders allow disks to be recorded that can contain **high definition** (**HD**) pictures and movies. Although Blu-ray® disks are the same physical size and shape as DVDs they can hold much more data.

Digital cameras have different maximum **image resolutions**. The more expensive cameras have higher resolutions.

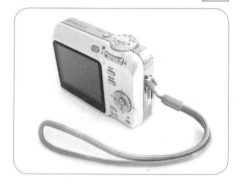

Pixels

Digital images are made up of many millions of tiny dots.

The resolution of an image is a measure of the number of dots or **pixels** that can be displayed in a given area.

The word 'pixel' is a shortened form of the words **picture element**. A pixel is the smallest amount of information that can be displayed on a screen, that is, a single coloured dot. Each dot can have its own colour. Monitors can display millions of different colours. (Look at the screen you are using through a magnifying glass. You should be able to see the individual pixels.)

The greater the number of pixels used in a given area the higher the resolution of the image.

More photos can be stored in a camera if a low resolution is selected, but the quality will not be as good as with a high resolution setting.

We use the unit **megapixels** when defining the area because many pixels are used in creating images. A megapixel is around one million pixels. That is 1000 pixels high by 1000 pixels wide. It is much easier to talk about a camera with a maximum resolution of 12 megapixels than one with a resolution of 12 000 000 pixels!

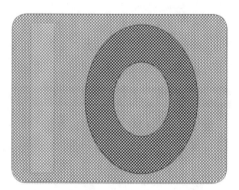

↑ **Images on screen are made of tiny dots called pixels**

Digital video camera

Revised

A digital video camera stores video clips as digital files in the camera. These can later be downloaded directly to a computer. Many video cameras also take still photos. You need a high definition camera to take HD movies. (HD stands for **high definition** and means that many more pixels are used per unit area than SD or **standard definition**.)

Digital photography	
Input devices	**Output devices**
● The digital camera ● Microphone	● Screen on the camera ● Speakers ● Printer

Flash memory

Revised

A flash memory card is a device that can slot into a camera, phone or computer and be used to save data. It does not need any power to keep the data stored which means that the memory cards can be taken from device to device or stored away from the device for long periods of time. They use the same technology as pen drives.

Display devices

Revised

The screen used on digital cameras is a liquid crystal display (LCD). Its display resolution is also measured in pixels or megapixels. The more pixels in a given area of screen, the clearer the image.

Photo-editing software

Revised

Once a picture is taken it will probably need to be edited. Editing might consist of cutting out parts you don't want, changing the brightness or contrast, or using some special editing features to change the way the image appears, such as distorting it in some way.

Some fashion magazines have been accused of editing images of models to make them look taller and thinner than they really are.

Special programs can be purchased to carry out the editing. Some simple picture editors (editing software) are usually supplied when you buy a computer or printer as part of the 'bundle', but you would have to spend many hundreds of pounds for a good professional editor.

Check your understanding

Tested

1 Give **one** difference between digital photography and traditional photography.

2 Explain what is meant by a pixel.

3 Image A has a resolution of 1000 × 1000.

   Image B has a resolution of 2000 × 400.

   a) Write down how many megapixels each image has.

   b) Which image has the higher resolution?

4 Describe **three** uses of a digital image.

5 State **two** output devices for a digital camera.

Go online for answers

Online

ICT and leisure services

Webcam

A **webcam** is a digital video camera connected directly to a computer. Webcams are sometimes found built into the lid of a laptop or into a computer monitor. Phone cameras can act like webcams.

Webcam	
Advantages	**Disadvantages**
A webcam could be used to ● monitor your home for security ● view your baby so you can check its welfare while you are in a different room ● send pictures of yourself to friends or relatives immediately ● monitor remote places without a human presence.	● You might not be aware that a webcam is taking pictures. ● You could be tempted to send a picture which you would later regret. ● Your privacy could be compromised.

> **Exam tip**
>
> Think of the input and output devices associated with different services. For webcam services these might include webcam and microphone for input and monitor and speaker for output.

Social networking

There are many social networking sites, such as Facebook, Instagram, Twitter.

Social networking	
Advantages	**Disadvantages**
● Usually free. ● Allows you to communicate with people who have similar interests. ● Easy to display your photos, achievements and so on. ● Easy to make friends online or keep in touch with old friends. ● Long-lost friends can be traced.	● People may not be who they say they are. ● It is tempting to reveal something, such as an embarrassing photograph, which you will later regret. ● Online bullying can take place. ● Sometimes employers check on social networking sites to see what kind of person you are in private.

Dangers of social networking

Be careful when you

● join a social network – be careful about how much **personal information** you give away when you sign up

● use a social network – do not arrange to meet somebody you have only ever met online.

If you feel uncomfortable or worried, tell somebody such as a parent or teacher.

↑ Dangers of social websites

Music and sound

Revised

Music can be obtained from a number of ICT sources, such as

- digital TV
- digital audio broadcasting (DAB)
- the internet
- CDs.

You can use a computer to listen to radio stations located almost anywhere in the world.

Some musical instruments can be connected to a computer using a **Musical Instrument Digital Interface** (**MIDI**) interface.

> **Exam tip**
>
> Music can be saved in a compressed format called MP3, which makes the files smaller and faster to download, although with a reduction in quality.

> **Exam tip**
>
> **Copyright law** protects original work, such as music accessed online. If you download music illegally you may be prosecuted and fined.

Music and sound	
Advantages	**Disadvantages**
<ul><li>Huge numbers of songs and videos can be stored in a very small space.</li><li>Almost any kind of music can be found.</li><li>Software can record the notes played on instruments thereby helping composers.</li></ul>	<ul><li>Music may be illegally copied on to a system.</li><li>Record companies may lose business or even fail because too many people copy the music instead of buying it.</li><li>Music produced electronically may not sound the same as listening to live music.</li></ul>

Mobile phones

Revised

Mobile phones today can be used for many things other than for talking to somebody. As such they are often called 'smart phones'. As well as all the normal phone functions, smart phones can be used to take pictures, access websites and play music. They can also be used as calendars, address books and to play games.

> **Exam tip**
>
> WAP stands for Wireless Application Profile. WAP phones can access the internet and view web pages.

Smart phones	
Advantages	**Disadvantages**
<ul><li>You can ring from anywhere there is cell phone signal coverage.</li><li>A smart phone is very compact and easy to carry around.</li><li>You can access the internet (if you have a WAP phone or wireless internet access).</li><li>People who are constantly on the move can easily be contacted.</li><li>It can avoid the need to make expensive calls from phones in hotels.</li><li>You can send and receive emails, text messages, pictures etc. while on the move.</li></ul>	<ul><li>They can be a nuisance to others when used in public.</li><li>They can be expensive, especially when used abroad or on an unsuitable tariff.</li><li>They might cause health problems with over-use or by living too near to a mobile phone transmitter mast.</li><li>They do not work if out of reach of a transmitter/receiver.</li><li>People can be contacted at any time, even when it is inconvenient.</li><li>People use mobile phones in cars without hands-free kits, which is illegal, very dangerous and can lead to accidents.</li><li>Mobile phone signals can interfere with electronic equipment, such as in hospitals or aeroplanes.</li></ul>

Augmented reality systems

Revised

Augmented reality (AR) systems place a computer-generated image onto a real-world view, which gives the user a composite image of whatever they are looking at. An example would be wearing special glasses that superimposed street names, or other information, on the view ahead, as you walked through a town. Smart phones can be used to play AR games. The image of the real world as seen through the phone may be overlaid with an imaginary creature that the user can 'catch' and score points.

Virtual reality

Revised

Virtual reality (VR) places the user in a completely imaginary world generated by computers. Using special equipment such as a VR helmet or gloves, the user can interact with the imaginary environment.

Augmented and virtual reality systems	
Advantages	**Disadvantages**
● Learning a skill without the expense of danger that may be involved in the real thing ● Ability to change conditions to suit circumstances	● Encourages people to become 'couch potatoes' and stay in, thus is bad for their health ● Possibility of loss of privacy

Check your understanding

Tested

1 List **three** advantages and **two** disadvantages of using webcams.

2 Copy and complete the table below. (The first two have been filled in for you.)

Input and output devices		
Service	**Input device**	**Output device**
Social networking	Webcam	Monitor
Mobile phones		
Music and sound		

3 Explain the dangers of giving away too many personal details on a social networking site.

Go online for answers

Online

How computers connect to the internet

The internet

Revised

The internet is a global network of computers. All computers on the internet can communicate with each other.

To use the internet you must subscribe to an **Internet Service Provider** (**ISP**). The ISPs (such as TalkTalk, Orange, AOL) have powerful computers called **servers** that are permanently connected to the internet. You link to them and they link you to the internet.

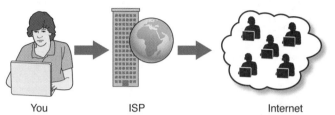

| You | ISP | Internet |

↑ **How computers connect to the internet**

Broadband

Revised

Broadband uses digital signals so there is no need for a modem. Connection is by **Asymmetric Digital Subscriber Line** (**ADSL**), for example using copper cables or optical fibres.

Unlike optical fibre, copper wires use electricity and need repeaters to boost the signal. The signals are prone to electrical interference (such as lightning).

> **Exam tip**
>
> The 'asymmetric' in ADSL means that downloading data is much faster than uploading data. This makes this very suitable for web browsing.

Broadband internet connectivity	
Advantages	**Disadvantages**
● You can download a lot of data quickly. ● It is possible to use the phone and internet at the same time. ● There is no need to dial-up. ● Several computers can use the same connection.	● As local usage increases, the download or upload times increase. ● As the distance from the exchange increases, the download and upload times increase. ● There is a greater risk of hacking.

Fibre-optic cables use light, so signals are able to travel long distances without getting weaker.

Fibre-optic internet connectivity	
Advantages	**Disadvantages**
● It provides a constant high speed link. ● It can also be used for television and interactive services. ● It is very reliable.	● It is expensive to install the cables. ● The cables do not reach everyone's home yet.

Wireless or **mobile** broadband allows you to use your laptop anywhere you can find a signal. You can fit a **dongle** to your computer via the USB port that will allow you to connect wirelessly to the internet using an ISP. However, most laptop computers have built-in wireless technology. You will need a 'hot spot' broadcasting nearby and permission to use the hot spot. You will find hotspots in airports, hotels, schools or almost anywhere in built-up areas.

802.11 wireless internet connectivity	
Advantages	**Disadvantages**
● There is no need for cables. ● It gives you internet connectivity on the move.	● The connectivity distance from the wireless access point is limited. ● There is a greater risk of hacking.

Satellite broadband connectivity does not require cables so it suits users who live far from telephone lines. The computer links to a satellite in geostationary orbit using signals sent to and from an aerial connected to the computer.

Exam tip

A satellite in geostationary orbit stays above the same point on the Earth's surface all the time.

Satellite internet connectivity	
Advantages	**Disadvantages**
● There is no need for expensive cables. ● It is ideal for locations where there is no telephone line.	● It requires a line-of-sight signal path to the satellite. ● It can be difficult with some interactive games because of signal lag. ● Connection and usage charges can be high.

Equipment connectivity   Revised

Bluetooth® is a wireless technology that allows all kinds of gadgets, such as Personal Digital Assistants (PDAs), smart phones, laptop computers, mice and keyboards, etc. to share information. Some examples are sharing music on your MP3 player with a car radio, or printing from your mobile phone.

Bluetooth® works wirelessly, but only in a very limited area, known as your **personal area network** (**PAN**), of up to 10 metres. For devices to communicate using Bluetooth® each must contain Bluetooth® technology.

Geographical Information Systems   Revised

A **Geographical Information System** (**GIS**) uses a combination of hardware, software and data to manage, analyse and display all kinds of geographical data. This can be shown in the form of maps, charts or reports. A GIS can be used in many ways within archaeology, land surveying, agriculture, etc.

Check your understanding   Tested

1 Name **four** different ways of connecting to the internet.

2 Describe **two** differences between fibre-optic cables and copper cables for connecting to the internet.

3 State **two** uses of a Geographical Information System (GIS).

4 Explain the advantages and disadvantages of using Bluetooth to connect devices.

5 John wants to watch a video online. Explain why fibre-optic cable is better than dial-up for this activity.

Go online for answers   Online

E-commerce

Online shopping

Revised

Shopping can be done from your own home using the internet.

E-commerce is the term used for buying or selling goods or services over the internet.

To carry out online shopping you

- use the internet to browse websites which sell what you want to buy
- search a website for your items
- add the items you want to buy to a 'shopping basket'
- proceed to a 'checkout'
- choose a method of payment
- enter the details of a credit or debit card
- enter address information of where the goods are to be delivered.

> **Exam tip**
>
> Learn the difference between a **credit card** and a **debit card**. With a credit card a company lends you money to buy the item and you pay them back at a later date. With a debit card you already have the money and the shop takes it from your bank straight away.

Online shopping	
Advantages to the customer	**Advantages to the business**
<ul><li>The range of goods available is very large.</li><li>Saves the time and expense of travelling to the shops.</li><li>Goods are delivered directly to your home saving you having to carry large, heavy items.</li><li>Price comparison websites and online reviews help you to make a better choice.</li><li>Benefits those who live far from shops, who have difficulty in travelling or who work at home or have very young children.</li></ul>	<ul><li>May not have to pay for premises such as an office or a shop (although you will still need a warehouse).</li><li>Can sell worldwide.</li></ul>
Disadvantages to the customer	**Disadvantages to the business**
<ul><li>May have to wait some time before an item arrives.</li><li>You can see only a picture of an item so you cannot touch, smell or examine it.</li><li>Food may no longer be fresh when it arrives. Fruit, eggs, etc. may be damaged in transit.</li><li>Need to have a debit or credit card, therefore it excludes young people and those with no bank account or poor credit ratings.</li><li>May have to pay high postage and packing/delivery charges.</li></ul>	<ul><li>Need to maintain an up-to-date website.</li><li>Extensive precautions must be taken to make sure the customer and payment details are not intercepted during the transaction.</li><li>Often have to rely on another company to deliver the goods.</li></ul>

Searching for products on websites

Revised

Searching for items on the internet can be difficult. When you search you should use a careful choice of words.

If you are using a phrase such as 'Holiday in Spain' you get around 40 000 000 sites (you get all sites with the word 'holiday' and all sites with the word 'Spain' in). If you search for the phrase 'Holidays in Spain' you can cut it down to 300 000. By being even more specific and searching 'Holidays in Spain 2011' you get 20 000. 'Cheap holidays in Spain 2011' would bring the number of sites appearing down to seven.

Booking online

To carry out online booking you would

- use the internet to find the website that provides what you want (e.g. 'Cheap holidays in Spain 2011')
- search the website for your specific requirements (e.g. self catering, near beach)
- choose the date, number of people, number of rooms and so on
- proceed to a 'checkout'
- choose a method of payment
- enter the details of credit or debit card
- enter information about the address where the tickets are to be delivered (sometimes you print off your tickets and travel plans yourself or they are sent to you by email).

You can book online for concerts, theatres, sporting events, holidays, flights and many other things.

> **Exam tip**
>
> A booking system is based around a database which stores the bookings and holds details of all the possible bookings that are available. The customer can search the database to find out which bookings can still be made.

Online booking	
Advantages to the customer	**Advantages to the business**
<ul><li>There should be no double-booking.</li><li>There is a fast response or even instant response to queries.</li><li>A booking can be made at any time of day or from anywhere in the world.</li><li>It is often cheaper to book online.</li><li>There is less chance of an error since you are filling in the data yourself.</li><li>There are often links to reviews or customers' ratings.</li></ul>	<ul><li>No high street shops are needed.</li><li>It attracts customers that are not local.</li></ul>
Disadvantages to the customer	**Disadvantages to the business**
<ul><li>Not everyone has the facilities or the ability to book online.</li><li>You must have a credit or debit card, or use a service like Paypal for most online bookings.</li></ul>	<ul><li>Initial costs of buying and installing the system will be high.</li><li>Agencies may close because customers are buying online.</li><li>People create their own tours so package holiday firms have to close through lack of customers.</li></ul>

Online accounts

When booking online you usually have to set up an account. You have to provide a **user name**, a **password** and an **email address**. The password and email addresses are often verified to make sure you have entered them correctly. This process involves you entering the information a second time. The computer checks your first entry with your second entry. The process is known as **verification**.

> **Exam tip**
>
> Verification can only test that the data has been entered accurately.

Check your understanding

1 Describe the term **e-commerce**.

2 List the processes involved in booking a holiday online.

3 Give **three** advantages to the customer of shopping online.

4 An online shopping account is being set up and a password has to be verified. Explain the process of **verification**.

Go online for answers

Online

Using ICT in schools

Registration systems

Schools have to take a register of pupils by law to know who is present and who is absent. Many schools use ICT to help record the attendance of pupils. This is known as **e-registration** (electronic registration).

Using e-registration, the pupil attendance is recorded on the computer system. This data can be used to

- show which pupils are absent from school
- find whether there are abnormal patterns of absence
- know exactly where each pupil is if an emergency arises
- know the reason why a pupil is absent.

There are a number of different systems in use.

- A **swipe card** system, where each pupil carries a card that they swipe through a card reader at each lesson.
- An **Optical Mark Reader** (**OMR**) system to input attendance from sheets marked by the teacher.
- A laptop is connected to the school network to register the pupils electronically as they come to class.
- **Finger print** system which can recognise pupils' individual finger prints.

Statistics can be worked out by the computer software for attendance, truancy and other absence.

↑ **Reporting for electronic registration**

Management Information Systems

A **Management Information System** (**MIS**) helps to organise data and present it in a form that can be used by the school management for a wide range of administrative tasks.

The benefit of using computers in school administration is that jobs can be completed faster and in an organised manner, and the results can be stored in such a way as to be useful later on.

A **database** stores pupil details such as

- personal details (name, date of birth, nationality, religion, etc.)
- home details (address, telephone number, etc.)
- contact details (name and emergency contact telephone number)
- school details (date of joining school, class, class tutor, etc.).

Other fields may include details about how the pupil travels to school, whether they have school dinners, and any medical problems the pupil might have.

A database can be searched

- to produce class lists
- to find the contact details of a pupil
- to find the results of assessments or exams
- to produce lists of failing pupils (or excellent ones!).

> **Exam tip**
>
> Be certain that you know the difference between a **database** and a **spreadsheet**. A database is used for storing data and producing useful reports. A spreadsheet is used for anything involving formulas and numerical calculations.

Databases might also be used for

- tracking orders and invoices
- administering pupil entries for exams
- recording books and book loans in the school library
- producing an inventory of all items the school has bought.

A **spreadsheet** could be used to plan and track the school budget helping to keep the total expenditure within fixed limits.

A **word processor** could be used to prepare letters to parents.

A school **intranet** may have a number of useful web pages for pupils, staff and parents.

Timetables
Revised

Creating a school timetable is very difficult and complex.

Using a computer and appropriate software to juggle the teachers, classrooms, subjects and pupils makes producing the school timetable more manageable. Once the timetable has been produced, the fact that all the data is stored in a computer makes producing lists such as individual pupil timetables much easier.

School events
Revised

ICT can help with organising school events.

End-of term show

- A database could store details of all the pupils taking part.
- A spreadsheet could help with the financial planning to make sure that the show makes an overall profit.
- Desktop publishing (DTP) software could be used to design advertising posters or produce the tickets and programmes.
- A word processor could be used to produce weekly rehearsal sheets showing the times of the rehearsals.
- A website about the show could be placed on the school intranet.
- MIDI could be used with musical instruments to record sound tracks.
- Computer-controlled lighting boards and sound systems might be used for the show.

School trip

- The internet could be used to find details of the destination and maps to get there.
- A database could be used to record the details of those going.
- A spreadsheet could be used to track income and expenditure.
- A word processor could be used to write to the parents about the trip.
- DTP software could be used to produce posters and leaflets about the trip.

Exam tip

When you write answers in an exam never use abbreviations for something the first time you mention it in your answer. For instance if using MIS always write Management Information System, or for OMR write Optical Mark Reader. After you have mentioned it once you can use the abbreviation.

Check your understanding
Tested

1 Write down what the following letters stand for.

   a) MIS   **b)** OMR   **c)** DTP   **d)** ICT   **e)** e-registration

2 Explain how OMR can be used in a school registration system.

3 List **five** ways a database could be used in school management.

4 Give **two** advantages for using computers to help produce the school timetable.

Go online for answers
Online

Data logging and control

Data logging

Data logging allows you to record a series of measurements taken by **sensors** made during an investigation.

Sensors are devices that measure quantities such as

- temperature
- light
- sound
- movement.

The data can be recorded automatically directly to a computer or you can **log** the data **manually** using a keyboard, mouse or microphone for later use.

The measurements from sensors can be taken at regular intervals and input to the computer.

Software in the computer can carry out an analysis or produce graphs with the data provided by the input from the sensors.

```
Sensors read  →  The computer  →  Graphs or tables
the data         processes the     can be printed
                 data
                   ↕
                 The data and
                 results can
                 be stored
```

Data logging systems	
Advantages	**Disadvantage**
<ul><li>Data collection can be automatic so no human presence is necessary.</li><li>Readings can be continually taken over long periods.</li><li>There is no chance of somebody forgetting to take a reading.</li><li>Readings will be more accurate if a computer takes them because there is no chance of human error.</li><li>Sensors can be placed in locations where it is dangerous for humans to go.</li><li>Readings can be taken very quickly (several readings every second from a number of different sensors). Humans could not achieve this.</li></ul>	<ul><li>If there is a fault it may go unnoticed for a long time.</li></ul>

Weather forecasting

Weather is always in the news. Bad weather, such as hurricanes, heavy snow or rainfall can affect millions of people and cause untold damage. Governments spend millions of pounds trying to forecast the weather to minimise the effects.

Some of the world's most powerful computers are used to forecast the weather and forecasts are becoming more accurate.

Computers are used to monitor

- the change in the average temperature of the Earth's surface (global warming)
- the ocean temperatures and currents
- the movement of areas of high and low pressures
- the paths of hurricanes.

Many millions of items of data are collected daily from all round the world. The data may consist of readings of temperature, humidity, atmospheric pressure, rainfall, visibility, or even radar data or infrared levels.

Sensors are used to collect this data from

- weather stations all round the world
- satellites
- weather balloons
- aircraft
- radar stations
- weather ships
- weather buoys permanently anchored out at sea.

Weather forecasting	
Advantages	**Disadvantages**
<ul><li>Farmers can know when to plant or harvest their crops.</li><li>People can choose where and when to take their holidays to take advantage of good weather.</li><li>Surfers know when large waves are expected.</li><li>Regions can be evacuated if hurricanes or floods are expected.</li><li>Aircraft and shipping rely heavily on accurate weather forecasting.</li></ul>	<ul><li>Weather is extremely difficult to forecast correctly.</li><li>It is expensive to monitor – so many variables from so many sources.</li><li>The computers needed to perform the millions of calculations necessary are expensive.</li><li>The weather forecasters get blamed if the weather is different from the forecast.</li></ul>

Microprocessor control

Revised

Microprocessors are the heart of computers, carrying out many of the functions of the **central processing unit** (**CPU**). Microprocessors are also contained in many electrical appliances in the home and at school. Some examples are

- central heating systems
- fire alarms
- dishwashers
- microwave ovens
- mobile phones
- games consoles
- televisions
- digital cameras
- burglar alarms
- washing machines
- DVD or Blu-ray recorders/players
- refrigerators/freezers
- Personal Digital Assistants (PDAs)
- MP3/MP4 players
- remote-control toys

Check your understanding

Tested

1 Complete the table using the following words.

   movement light temperature sound

Situation	Sensor measuring
Measuring a cooling liquid every 10 seconds	
Seeing how often animals use a woodland path	
The amount of noise aircraft make	
Automatically open curtains when the sun rises	

2 State **three** ways of entering data manually.

3 Give **three** advantages of data logging.

4 State **four** ways of collecting data to use for weather forecasting.

5 Weather forecasting uses ICT. ICT is also used by us to access the weather forecasts.

   Describe **four** ways ICT allows us to access the weather forecast. In addition, point out **at least four** advantages or disadvantages of forecasting the weather, including **at least one** of each.

   (Remember that the quality of written communication will be assessed in longer questions such as this one.)

Go online for answers

Online

Learning with ICT

There are many ways ICT can help with learning.

Interactive whiteboards (IWB)
Revised

- Large white screens are connected to a computer and used like a computer screen. A special pen is used like a mouse pointer. These help make learning interactive.

Computer-assisted learning (CAL)
Revised

- A way to learn a skill using a computer and interactive software on CD or DVD, or by using the internet. Using CAL programs can be a more enjoyable way to learn than traditional methods.

Internet
Revised

- The **internet** can help with research.
- A **discussion group** on the internet (often called a **bulletin board** or a **forum**) can be helpful in getting ideas.
- **Email** can provide contact with pupils in other schools.

Application software
Revised

- **Desktop Publishing (DTP)** software can help with the presentation of coursework or other tasks.
- **Spreadsheets** can be used to create charts and organise numerical data.
- **Databases** can be used to store, sort or search data and produce reports.

Distance learning
Revised

Distance learning is a means of studying for a qualification from home by learning online, using web pages and other resources, and then taking online examinations.

Distance learning	
Advantages	**Disadvantages**
• You can learn from anywhere, no matter how remote. • Learning can be done in your own time and at your own speed. • There are often online chat rooms or discussion forums where others who are learning the same subject can exchange ideas or discuss problems. • There is a wide range of learning courses available.	• Problems may not easily be solved because there is no tutor to discuss them with. • Students may feel isolated. • There may be a lack of motivation if the student can select the frequency and times when learning takes place.

A computer attached to a network or the internet allows us to have access to a great range of educational services for distance learning. Some of these are

● Online tutorials – the internet provides many online tutorials which may be animated and interactive. BBC Bitesize is a website that provides a resource for pupils studying for GCSEs.

Online tutorials	
Advantages	**Disadvantages**
● They are readily available. ● No teacher is required. ● Questions can be quickly answered. ● On-screen demonstrations can be given.	● You cannot ask a teacher questions so easily. ● You cannot usually skip bits you already know. ● They often proceed at a steady speed that may not suit you.

● Online assessment – often associated with distance learning or online tutorials. Questions are presented on screen and the pupil answers using the keyboard or mouse. The marks may be immediately available.

Online assessment	
Advantages	**Disadvantages**
● Tests can be taken any time. ● Reduced wastage of paper and other resources. ● Results are available immediately or very quickly. ● Records of mistakes, marks given and time taken on questions allows detailed statistics to be produced.	● It is an impersonal way of testing. ● Is expensive and difficult to set the questions. ● Very hard to mark subjective answers such as essays. ● Takes a lot of organisation and may need a lot of computers for a large class.

● Virtual Learning Environment (VLE) – can offer a complete educational course online without a teacher needing to be present. It provides a set of tools that allows a teacher to set up learning material, links and feedback to teach a particular topic. Working at a computer, a pupil is able to proceed through a lesson or series of lessons at their own pace.

Virtual Learning Environment	
Advantages	**Disadvantages**
● Learning can take place at any time. ● A teacher does not need to be present. ● A variety of text, graphics, audio and visual sources can be used.	● Answers to questions may take a long time to arrive. ● Material may become out of date. ● Training to use the VLE could use up valuable learning time. ● Equipment can fail leaving the pupil without a lesson.

● Massive open online courses (MOOCs) – online courses run by universities and colleges around the world, in which anyone can enrol. They are often free of charge, with a charge sometimes being made for a certificate of participation.

Massive open online courses (MOOCs)	
Advantages	**Disadvantages**
● Help to enhance a person's career and education ● Allow people to learn new skills online at home without undue expense ● High-quality courses delivered by respected institutions	● Hard to keep motivated on online courses ● Personal interaction is missing ● Language can be a barrier, as courses are often given in the native language of the institution delivering the course

Check your understanding — Tested

1 Expand the following.

a) VLE   b) IWB   c) CAL

2 Explain **four** ways ICT can help in the classroom.

3 Explain why distance learning can be an advantage to a student.

Go online for answers — Online

The desktop environment

Desktop

Revised

When you switch on your computer and the system is ready to use, the screen displays a virtual **desktop**. A desktop is an example of a **Graphical User Interface** (**GUI**). A **desktop environment** (**DTE**) contains **icons**, **windows**, **toolbars** and **folders**.

Microsoft Windows is an example of a GUI that uses Windows, Icons, Menus and a Pointer. This is sometimes called the WIMP environment.

To move a pointer around the screen we can use a device such as a joystick, touch pad, tracker ball or, most commonly, a mouse.

The DTE can be **customised** to your requirements.

- Icon size – This can be changed to suit your needs. You may have a lot of icons displayed, in which case you may want them small, or you may have poor eyesight, in which case you need them larger.
- Window size – This can be changed by using a mouse to drag the edges in the direction you wish to increase or decrease the size.
- Mouse settings – Individuals are different and people have different speeds of reactions, so you may wish to change the settings for the mouse you are using. It is usually possible to change

  - the double-click speed
  - whether it is for a left-handed or right-handed person
  - the pointer speed
  - pointer trails
  - the size and shape of the pointer.

- Other changes you can make to the display are

  - the screen resolution, which changes the number of pixels on the screen. The more pixels the more detailed the images
  - the desktop fonts, which changes the size or number of dots per inch (dpi) to make your fonts more readable
  - the colours of almost anything
  - the position of the icons and windows
  - the graphics which are displayed when you login
  - the screen contrast and volume settings.

Files and folders

Revised

Saved data is usually referred to as a **file**. A file may contain text, numbers, an image, a video or sound. It is possible to **move** a file from one **folder** to another, or even move a representation of it around on the desktop. Files and folders can be **copied**, **deleted** or **renamed**.

Exam tip

Files and folders should always be given names that describe what they contain, not who created them or why or when they were created.

On-screen help

Revised

On-screen help is usually built in to the application you are using. Help is often accessed by pressing a **shortcut** key, such as F1, or by clicking on the question mark on the menu bar. Some applications have a search facility where you type a **key word** or two describing what you need help with. If the computer is connected to the internet, then the search for help may also produce answers from other users of the package.

Control panel

Revised

The control panel of a computer is a collection of all the useful programs that can be used to change the environment of your computer to suit you.

Print settings

Revised

A menu of options is often offered when something is printed. Options may include

- which pages to print (e.g. all the pages, the current page, a selection)
- the number of copies to print
- which printer to use (e.g. you may have a choice of colour printer, photocopier or laser printer).

Password protection

Revised

If you are leaving your computer logged in for any reason, it is important to make sure that your work is secure and that no-one other than you can access your work area. You will need a password to unlock it again.

Shortcuts

Revised

Shortcuts allow a complex series of actions to be carried out by doing a mouse click or pressing a key or combination of keys. There are many shortcuts and some are shown in the table. They depend on which operating system or type of software you are using. The ones shown are for Microsoft products.

Shortcut	Action
Double click on an icon on the desktop.	The application runs or the folder opens.
Press F1 (function key 1).	A search box opens.
Control + escape.	Displays the Start menu.
Right click mouse.	A pop-up menu associated with the object appears.
Control + B.	Highlighted text becomes bold.

Check your understanding

Tested

1 Match these words to the statements below.

   shortcut   file   GUI   icon

   a) Saved data containing text, numbers, an image, a video or sound.

   b) A key that allows a complex action to be undertaken.

   c) A small image representing a file.

   d) A type of user interface.

2 Fill in the gaps in this sentence.

   An environment that uses W_____, I_____, M_____ and P_____ is often known as a WIMP environment.

3 It is possible to change the resolution of the screen. Explain what this means.

Go online for answers

Online

Software

Sources of information

Information can be retrieved from a number of sources for many different purposes. Different sources are suitable for different needs.

Information can come from

- Files on **disks** or **memory sticks**. This kind of information is often personal, such as an address book or sets of holiday photographs.
- **CD-ROMs** and **DVDs** can contain encyclopaedias, catalogues, videos, songs, clip art collections and so on.
- **SD cards** are used to store information in devices such as digital cameras and motor vehicle dashcams.
- **Cloud storage** can store data on remote servers anywhere in the world. The data on the cloud can be accessed from any device, provided you have the correct user ID and password. Unlike physical devices such as laptops, the storage is effectively unlimited.
- **Databases** in schools and businesses contain useful information that can allow staff to quickly find information such as contact details or details of an order.
- **Websites** are a valuable source of information, but be careful not to be led astray by sites that are not up to date or those that may provide incorrect information. Websites run by well known organisations or governments can usually be trusted to hold reliable information.

Once we have the information we can present it in a number of ways using different types of applications software.

> **Exam tip**
>
> If you are asked for an example of applications software in an examination always use the generic terms. For example, if you are asked for an example of software that can be used to write a letter, use the answer 'word processor'. If you use 'Word' or some other proprietary name you will get no marks.

The purpose and use of applications software

- **Word processors** can be used for writing assignments, producing letters, keeping notes or writing books and other word-processing tasks.
- **Desktop publishers** can be used to manipulate text and images to produce posters, leaflets, newsletters and other similar documents.
- **Presentation software** can be used to produce slides used in teaching or lecturing, and may include video, sound, animations and slide transitions. Some of the slides may have **hyperlinks** to other slides within the presentation, other presentations, other programs, music files, websites, etc. There are many possibilities.
- **Spreadsheets** can be used to perform calculations. Provided the formula is correct, the calculations will always be accurate. Models of situations can be undertaken and 'What if?' questions can be asked. Charts and graphs can be drawn from the data to illustrate results of an investigation.
- **Databases** are used for storing data which than then be sorted or searched. Reports can be printed out.

> **Exam tip**
>
> A slide transition is the way one slide changes to another. This can be in different ways, such as 'dissolve', 'wedge', 'wipe down' or 'fade smoothly', and many others.

Using ICT to support learning disabilities

ICT can help pupils with their learning. Software has been developed to help with

- learning difficulties to improve reading or writing skills
- basic mathematics skills
- accessing a computer, if the pupil has a visual impairment
- typing by using predictive text.

Desktop environments

Desktop environments can be customised as shown on page 24 for those with visual or motor impairments.

Voice recognition software

People who have difficulty typing can use a **microphone** as an input device to issue commands to a computer or to use the applications available. Specialist software will convert the user's voice into words on the computer.

Predictive software can offer choices of words or phrases that can be selected to speed up text input.

Text-to-voice software

Those who have difficulty seeing the text on a screen can use **text-to-voice** software. This software takes the text from the screen and uses **synthesised speech** to read out whatever is on the screen using a speaker.

Braille keyboards

Braille keyboards are input devices for those that cannot see the keyboard, though most people can be trained to become touch typists. A Braille keyboard has raised dots for the key character on the key.

Touch sensitive data entry devices

Some devices work by a user touching them. The position where the device is touched is sensed and used as data. A touch screen might have a menu displayed on it. The user selects an option by touching the screen at one of a number of predefined positions.

Concept keyboards

Concept keyboards are touch sensitive boards that have special overlays that help a handicapped person to input data. They have also been developed to help young people or those with learning difficulties.

Other uses of touch screens

Touch screens are often situated in places where members of the public can use them or where a mouse or keyboard could be lost or stolen. For example, they may be found in

- museums, describing exhibits
- banks, explaining to a customer the services the bank can offer
- doctors' surgeries to allow a patient to register their attendance without needing to see the receptionist
- restaurants or bars, where each item a customer buys is touched on a screen by a member of staff and the total bill is automatically calculated and displayed
- in factories, where dirt and grease could damage keyboards, and touch screens can be wiped clean easily
- in greenhouses or other places where there are liquids present or a damp or dirty atmosphere.

Touch screen	
Advantages	**Disadvantages**
• Low-level ICT skills are needed. • Little possibility of damage or theft.	• It may become dirty or scratched and difficult to read with use.

Check your understanding
Tested

1 For each of the following, state which application software would be most useful to complete the task.
   a) Writing a letter.
   b) Keeping an account of money coming in and out for a school trip.
   c) Making a poster.
   d) Giving a slide show about your skiing holiday.
   e) Keeping a record of your collection of DVDs.

2 Name **three** sources of information and for each give an example of the information you might collect from that source.

3 Give **four** uses of touch sensitive screens.

4 Describe the specialist software each of the following could use.
   a) A person who is unable to read words on a screen.
   b) A person who has difficulty typing.
   c) A person with learning difficulties.

Go online for answers
Online

Databases 1

Databases

Revised

A database is an organised collection of related data. It is possible to add, edit, manage and retrieve data from a database. The structure of a database allows data to be found and used quickly.

Data types

Revised

Data is stored in the computer in binary form as a series of 0s and 1s. In order to process the data the computer needs to know the **data type**. The common data types are shown below.

Data type	Example	Description
Number (integer)	43	A whole number (positive or negative but no fractions).
Number (Real)	432.51	Any number including whole numbers and fractions.
Text or string	John Smith	Letters, numbers or other characters such as punctuation marks.
Date/Time	04/10/06 12:23:09	Any time or date. The way the time or date is displayed depends on how it is formatted.
Currency	£12.50	Money (including foreign currencies such as $ or €).
Boolean	Yes	The data can have only two possible outcomes such as 'Yes' or 'No', 'True' or 'False', 'Male' or 'Female'.
Lists	Red Green Blue Yellow	The data is in the form of a list, sometimes called a 'drop-down' list. Only data from the list can be selected.
Picture		Image data from a digital camera, mobile phone, the internet, a clip-art library or scanned drawing.
Sound	A sound or music clip.	A beep from a bar code reader or a popular song.
Video	A moving picture.	A video introduction to a computer game or a downloaded film/TV programme.

Files, records, fields

Revised

- A **field** is a single data item.
- A **record** consists of a collection of related fields.
- A **file** is a collection of related records. In some databases they are referred to as **tables**.

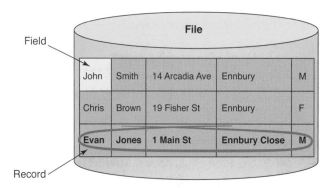

↑ **How files, records and fields are related**

Key field

Revised

A **key field** uniquely identifies a record. This means that no two records will have the same key field.

The purpose of the key field is to be able to refer to an individual record using a single field. This often takes the form of an identity number, member number or bar code.

Validation

Revised

Data entered into a database must be sensible or we get GIGO (see page 5). **Validation rules** are created to check that data being entered is sensible. As the data is entered, it is checked to see that it obeys the rules, and any data that does not, will not be accepted.

- A **range check** ensures that the data entered is within a sensible range.
- A **type check** ensures that the data is of the correct data type.
- A **length check** ensures that the length of the input for the number of characters is used.
- A **lookup list** checks the data entered against a limited number of possible entries.
- A **picture** or **format check** ensures that the data being entered has a particular pattern, such as a post code or a car registration number.
- An **input mask** is used to force the data to conform to a rule. The computer checks to see that the entry conforms to that pattern.
- A **presence check** ensures that certain data is present.

Reports

Revised

A **report** is a printed document that contains data from the database, organised and analysed in a certain way. Once a report has been created it can be saved and used again. A report from a student database might list the students in each class in alphabetical order.

Calculated fields

Revised

Not all data needed in a report may be present in a database. For example, a person's age is never included because it changes day by day. If you want to use age in a report it has to be calculated. The result is known as a **calculated field**.

A calculated field only exists in a database when it is needed, such as at the time of running a query or printing a report.

The field can be given a field name, but no data will be held permanently in the database.

Check your understanding

Tested

1 State the data type for each of the following.

   a) 23   **b)** Film star   **c)** ?@~   **d)** 14.23

2 Describe validation.

3 Identify the type of validation used to check

   a) a number between 0 and 100   **b)** Mr, Mrs, Miss, Dr, Rev   **c)** GL19 3ZX

Go online for answers   Online

Databases 2

Uses of a database

Revised

Databases can be used to

- **add**, **change** or **delete** records
- **search** for a particular record
- **sort** the records into a given order
- print **reports** about some aspect of the database
- use the data in other applications.

Updating records

Revised

Records do not stay the same for very long so they need to be **updated**.
For example, people get married and change their name; people move
and change their address; prices of goods change; or a school might

- add new records when a new pupil arrives
- edit existing records when a pupil moves house
- delete old records when a pupil leaves.

Sorting

Revised

Records often need to be **sorted** into order.

A teacher may want a list in

- **alphabetical order** to call the register
- order of examination marks to see who came top of the class
- **chronological order** of dates of birth to see who is the oldest.

Records can be sorted into **ascending** or **descending** order. Class
registers are listed in alphabetical ascending order, but exam marks are
usually in numerical descending order.

Interrogating a database

Revised

A database is searched by creating a **query** that specifies the fields you are
searching for and the fields that you would like displayed.

Sorting speeds up searching.

A **simple search** looks for data in one field only. This is sometimes called
a keyword search.

A **complex search** looks for data with **multiple criteria**.

The table shows a number of **operators** that can be used in searches.

Operator	Example	Result
=	Surname = Smith	All records with surname 'Smith'.
<	Date of Birth < 02/01/1998	Records of all born before 2 January 1998.
>	Surname > Smith	Records of those whose surnames come after Smith in the alphabet.
<>	Surname <> Smith	Records of those whose surname is not Smith.
AND	Surname = Smith AND Form = 10Y	Finds all the Smiths in form 10Y.
OR	Surname = Smith OR Form = 10Y	Finds the records of all the Smiths in the database as well as all the members of 10Y.

Wildcard characters and the logical operator LIKE

Revised

A **wildcard** is used in a query to stand for any character you do not know exactly. For instance to find all the surnames beginning with 'S' you might write: surname LIKE "S*".

Check online for other examples of the use of wildcards.

Using parameters

Revised

A parameter query is one where the actual item being searched for is not known, but will be added into the query when the database is being interrogated. For instance, if a database is being interrogated to find the record of a certain customer, the query will be designed to allow the customer ID to be entered at the time of the search. The customer ID is known as the **parameter** of the query.

Benefits of information handling

Revised

- Finding and editing data is much faster than in a paper-based system.
- Data entered can be validated to make sure that no inappropriate data gets into the database. This is sometimes called ensuring **data integrity**.
- Results of searches can be used to produce printed reports.
- Data in a database can be shared with other users on a network.
- Passwords may be set so that no unauthorised user can access the database.

Security and databases

Revised

If data is secure then

- it cannot be destroyed
- it cannot be accidentally or maliciously altered
- it cannot fall into the hands of unauthorised people.

A number of methods are used to keep data secure, such as **physical security**. Physical security includes

- locks on doors
- alarms
- ID cards
- **biometric** systems, such as finger print or voice recognition, iris scanning.

> **Exam tip**
>
> A biometric system is a security system that uses physical characteristics such as fingerprints, voice, facial features and eye scans to identify people. It serves the same purpose as a password. It proves you are who you say you are.

Passwords

Revised

Authorised users are given a user name. Each user also has a password that proves the user is really the one whose user name is given.

Using passwords is a method of **authentication**.

Access rights

Revised

Access rights can be placed on individual files to give

- no right to access the file
- read access, where the file can be viewed but not altered
- write access, allowing the user to alter the contents of the file.

Backup and recovery procedures

Revised

A **backup** is a second copy of the data. If a problem arises with the data file, then the back-up copy can be used instead. Backups are

- saved on removable media (CD, DVD, tape, memory stick)
- stored at a separate location in a locked room or fireproof safe
- made regularly (often every day).

Using the backup copies allows recovery of corrupt or lost data.

Check your understanding

Tested

1 List **four** benefits of using a database.

2 Describe **four** methods for keeping data secure.

3 Explain what is meant by a wildcard.

Go online for answers

Online

Communicating electronically

Email
Revised

Email is a system that allows a network or internet user to send a message to another person with an email account.

Email addresses are provided by an Internet Service Provider (ISP), for example

john.smith@myprovider.co.uk

Every email user has a unique email address.

To send an email you must include

- the email address or addresses
- the subject of the message
- the actual message
- an attachment (if you are sending one).

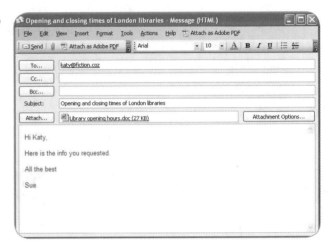

↑ **Email features**

Progress of an email
Revised

1 Log in
2 Open an email program.
3 Write the email text.
4 Send the email. (Email stays in your **outbox** until sent.)

Incoming mail goes into your **inbox**.

Email facilities
Revised

- **Address book** – allows you to store email addresses.
- You can create **groups** of addresses so a message can be sent to a group without having to type in all the individual email addresses.
- The emails you receive are stored in the **inbox folder**.
- You can also **reply** to an email and write a message back to the sender.
- You can **forward** an email to another user's address.
- The emails that are waiting to be sent are stored in the **outbox**.
- A record of all the emails that you have sent is in the **sent folder**.
- All the emails that you have deleted are stored in the **deleted item folder**. This folder is sometimes called the **bin**.
- You can send the same email to a number of different addresses.
  - Separate different addresses by commas or semi colons.
  - Use the **carbon copy** (**Cc**) address box.
  - If you don't want the others to know you have sent a copy, use the **blind carbon copy** (**Bcc**) box.
  - Put the name of a group in the address space.
- A document, picture, sound file or video clip can be **attached** to an email.
- A standard message can be set up to be attached to all your emails automatically. This might be your name, address and mobile number. It is known as a **signature**.

> **Exam tip**
>
> When asked for the advantages and disadvantages of email make sure that you give full sentences. Statements such as 'cheaper', 'quicker' and so on are useless on their own. You need to write statements such as 'An email is cheaper than post because you do not need to pay for an envelope and stamp'.

Email	
Advantages	**Disadvantages**
● Emails can arrive within seconds. ● It is a relatively cheap method of communication. ● The recipient does not need to be online when the email is sent. ● An email can be sent to a number of different users at the same time. ● Files may be attached to an email. ● Emails can be forwarded to others very easily.	● Objects, such as parcels, cannot be sent. ● A large amount of unwanted or **spam** emails are received. ● A paper document will need to be scanned before it can be sent by email. ● Some legal processes require original documents and will not accept emails. ● There is sometimes a limit to the size of an attached file.

Instant messaging

Revised

Images, songs and text can be shared using instant messaging. For example, most mobile phones allow Short Message Service (SMS) texts to be sent, often free of charge, although sending larger files such as media files may incur a charge.

Security

Revised

There are some **security** aspects associated with emails.

● A computer **virus** might be attached to the message.

● **Spam** (including of unwanted advertising) can quickly clutter up your system.

● **Phishing** emails pretend to come from an official organisation and ask for your personal and bank details that, if you reply, can be used to steal your money.

● Emails are sometimes used to send offensive and hurtful comments to someone. This is known as **cyber bullying**.

● **Encryption** scrambles a message using an encryption key, making it unintelligible to anyone who intercepts the data. Only a person with the decryption key can understand the message.

● **Distributed denial of service (DDOS)** tries to make an online service unavailable by bombarding it with messages from many sources.

● **Spoofing** is sending emails that appear to come from a known source, often asking for personal information; the return address is hidden or designed to look very much like the legitimate one. The hacker assumes that the email is likely to be opened, so it may contain a virus or trojan that can harm the user's files.

Check your understanding

Tested

1 State **three** different things you should include in an email.

2 Describe the security problems associated with emails.

3 Describe the difference between 'Cc' and 'Bcc' for emails.

4 Give **four** advantages of using email.

Go online for answers

Online

Calculations and modelling

Spreadsheet software

Spreadsheets are for manipulating numbers and doing calculations or for modelling real-life situations.

A spreadsheet can be used to

● carry out calculations

● ask 'What if?' questions

● produce graphs and charts.

A spreadsheet consists of **workbooks** which are divided into **worksheets**.

A worksheet consists of a grid of rectangular **cells** which can contain text, numbers and formulas.

> **Exam tip**
>
> Make sure you are absolutely clear that you know the difference between a spreadsheet application and a database application. Never confuse the two in an examination. If it is used for searching or sorting it is probably a database. If it is used for calculations it is probably a spreadsheet.

Cells

A **cell reference** always starts with a letter and ends with a number (for example, C5).

A **range** of cells is a set of cells in a column or row.

A **block** of cells may consist of several rows and columns.

Data entered into a cell can be of different **data types**, for example, text, number, currency, date, etc.

Each cell can contain

● **text** – anything not recognised by the spreadsheet as data used in a calculation

● **labels** – any text in a cell describing the data in that row or column

● **data** – any numbers that are entered for use in a calculation

● **formulas** and functions – mathematical calculations carried out automatically.

↑ **Spreadsheet terminology**

Formulas

Formulas appear in a **formula bar**.

The result of a formula is automatically recalculated every time the data on the spreadsheet is changed. An example of a formula is

=(B3*C3)+E4

Functions

Some common calculations are carried out using **functions**, for example

● **SUM** – Instead of entering the formula **=D4+D5+D6+D7**, you can enter the abbreviated formula **=SUM(D4:D7)**.

● **AVERAGE** – To find the average of a range of numbers stored in, say, cells B4:B10, use **=AVERAGE(B4:B10)**.

● **IF** – The IF function compares a cell with some data and produces one result if the comparison is true, another if it is false. An IF statement could show whether or not someone has passed an examination: **=IF(A1<10, "Fail", "Pass")**.

- **COUNT** – counts the number of cells that contain numbers. =COUNT(A1:A15) would count how many cells in the range A1 to A15 contained numbers.
- **COUNTA** – counts the number of cells that contain anything.
- **COUNTIF** – counts the number of cells that meet a certain criterion. =COUNTIF(A1:A15,"<5") finds the number of cells that contain values less than 5.

Formatting

Revised

The content of a cell can be **formatted** for

- font style
- size
- colour
- border style
- background colour.

Cells are often formatted to reflect the data that is to be held in them.

Data types you might use when formatting cells are

- currency
- number
- real
- integer (whole number)
- date
- text

Merging cells

Revised

Cells can be **merged** to make one larger cell. Cells in a spreadsheet cannot be split, but merging the cells above two cells will make it appear as if the cell below has been split.

	A	B	C	D	E	F	G
1							
2			Class Museum Trip				
3							
4							
5							
6							
7							
8							
9							

↑ **A group of cells (A1:G2) have been merged together**

Replicating cells

Revised

When you position the mouse pointer in the bottom right-hand corner of the cell and drag down or across, the spreadsheet tries to respond intelligently. If there is a formula in the cell the spreadsheet will try to adjust it as it as you drag to fit in with the new position and the cells being referred to.

Check your understanding

Tested

1 a) Identify cells from the spreadsheet shown here that contain the following
   i) a label
   ii) text
   iii) the range used to find the total selling price.
  b) Write down a formula involving SUM used for the total in cell F11.

	D	E	F	G
1	Gender	Date in	Price paid	Selling price
2	Female	11/08/2010	£5.00	£6.25
3	Female	18/05/2010	£5.00	£6.25
4	Female	09/09/2010	£1.10	£1.38
5	Male	04/03/2010	£1.42	£1.78
6	Male	17/04/2010	£7.50	£9.38
7	Female	29/06/2010	£7.72	£9.65
8	Male	11/10/2010	£4.12	£5.15
9	Female	19/06/2010	£8.31	£10.39
10	Male	10/09/2010	£3.63	£4.54
11		Totals	£43.80	£54.75

Go online for answers

Online

Cell referencing and charts

Cell referencing

When a formula is copied by 'filling down', the **cell references** in cells are adjusted as you drag the pointer down the page.

● Relative cell references

The cells D2, D3 and D4 now contain formulas that are **relative** to the rows they are in. The formulas are relative to their position in the spreadsheet.

● Absolute cell references

Sometimes it is important to use part of a formula that should not change when the formulas are copied. For example, if the rate of VAT was stored in B2 as 20%, then the 'B2' part of the formula must not change because the rate will be 20% for everything. All the other cell references will change.

When the formula is copied, the relative addresses change, but the absolute addresses do not.

Absolute cell references have a $ character in front of the letter and number that are required to stay the same. Think of the '$' as glue. It glues this absolute cell into every formula it is needed in.

	A	B	C	D
1	Item	Cost per item	Number	Total cost
2	Beans	£0.45	5	=B2*C2
3	Bread	£0.79	3	=B3*C3
4	Butter	£1.05	2	=B4*C4

↑ **Relative referencing**

	A	B	C	D
1	VAT rate	20%		
2	Item	Cost before VAT	VAT	Total cost
3	Bike	£145.00	=B3*B1	=B3+C3
4	TV	£259.00	=B4*B1	=B4+C4
5	Toaster	£15.99	=B5*B1	=B5+C5

↑ **Absolute referencing**

Charts and graphs

Using charts or graphs makes information easier to understand. Patterns and trends are easier to see.

Data can be **selected** on the spreadsheet and a chart or graph of this data can be created.

It is important to select the chart or graph that is most appropriate to illustrate the information.

● **Bar charts** are used to compare different values. The biggest bar or column shows the greatest value.

● **Pie charts** are used to show how a total is divided among a number of different categories.

● **Line graphs** display the trend of sequences of values by using plotted points.

> **Exam tip**
>
> A person should be able to clearly see what is being displayed on a graph or chart. You need to make sure all the axes, sectors, etc. are clearly labelled and that a sensible descriptive title is given.

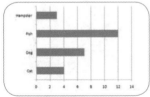

↑ **Bar chart**

↑ **Pie chart**

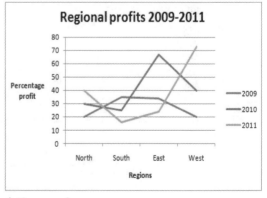

↑ **Line graph**

'What if?' calculations

Changing the data in a spreadsheet model allows you to make and test **predictions**. For example, you could explore what would happen to your profits if VAT changed to 25%. These are known as '**What if?**' calculations. They allow you to use the spreadsheet to see what would happen if you changed certain figures in the spreadsheet. Spreadsheets have a 'knock-on' ability. If you change one figure, all the figures in the spreadsheet associated with it will change too.

Benefits of using a spreadsheet

- **Automatic recalculation** – Every time the content of a cell is changed, calculations are performed and other cells are updated if necessary.
- **Graphs** and **charts** can be drawn using the data in selected cells. These have greater visual impact and are easier to understand than complex sheets of data. Trends and patterns are easier to see on graphs.
- **Replication** – Once the first formula is correctly entered, it is possible to drag across the adjacent cells in a row or column so the computer copies the pattern of the calculation.
- '**What if?**' calculations can be undertaken.
- **Formulas** can be stored and reused.
- **Calculations** involving large numbers are possible.

Check your understanding

1 Fill in the missing words.

If the cell reference changes when copying a formula, it is known as r_____ referencing. If the cell reference stays the same, it is known as a_____ referencing.

2 Explain the use of 'What if? calculations.

3 Choose the best type of chart for
   a) comparing the number of boys and girls present in a school each day for a week
   b) comparing the number of calories of five different foods.
   c) showing the attendance at a night club every Saturday for eight weeks to show the attendance trend.

Go online for answers

Control

Control systems
Revised ☐

ICT can be used to **control** and **monitor** many areas of our lives. In our homes, we might find a number of these devices, some of which we can control and some which monitor our environment. Some of these are **electronic toys** and **computer games**.

Central heating systems
Revised ☐

A central heating system is controlled by a microprocessor that has a number of sensors attached to it. The process follows a continuing cycle.

● Regular readings of temperature are input.
● The microprocessor analyses the reading.
● If the temperature is too hot, it switches off the heater. If the temperature is too cold, it switches on the heater.

A learning thermostat can learn when a house is occupied and unoccupied, and adjust the temperatures accordingly. It is linked to the internet and can be controlled from a mobile phone. It learns the user's habits and also checks the location of the user's phone.

Burglar alarms
Revised ☐

Burglar alarms are often very complex and use many sensors.

● Passive Infrared (PIR) sensors can detect movement in a room.
● Proximity sensors can be used on windows or doors to detect when they are opened.
● Pressure pads can be placed under mats to sense when someone stands on them.

If any sensor is activated a signal will be sent to an alarm bell or, sometimes, directly to a police station or security guard.

Smart meters
Revised ☐

Meters measure the amount of electricity, gas or water that is being used in a home. **Smart meters**

● take the readings at regular time intervals
● send the readings back to head office, so there is no need for human meter readers
● monitor when the greatest consumption of the resource is taking place
● help customers become more efficient in their use of the resource.

Security systems
Revised ☐

Many buildings, including houses, have smoke detectors and fire detection systems. These systems can

● activate a siren or bell
● set off an automatic sprinkler system
● send a message automatically to the fire station.

Controlling devices

Robots and other machines can be **programmed** to operate in a certain way. Some simple instructions, very similar to the instructions used by robots, can be found in the computer control language **LOGO**. LOGO is used in schools to move a symbol across a computer screen, but it can also be used to control the movements of a small robot (sometimes called a turtle).

Some of the instructions used are FORWARD, BACKWARD, PEN UP, PEN DOWN, RIGHT, LEFT. For example, the following could be used by a screen turtle.

- PEN DOWN – this lowers an imaginary pen and draws a line on the screen as the turtle moves.

- PEN UP – this lifts the imaginary pen so the line no longer shows on the screen.

- FORWARD 100 – this moves the turtle forward 100 units.

- RIGHT 90 – this turns the robot through 90 degrees.

START
PEN DOWN
FORWARD 100
RIGHT 90
FORWARD 100
PEN UP
FORWARD 100
PEN DOWN
FORWARD 50
STOP

↑ **Logo program and the track it produces**

If you imagine that the 'pen' in the program shown here was a laser beam cutting steel and the turtle was a robot cutter, then you get the idea of how industrial robots operate.

Computer control	
Advantages	**Disadvantages**
● Robots do not require payment. ● Robots never need to take a holiday, report in sick or go on strike. ● They can operate in conditions that would be dangerous to a person such as near a furnace or in an environment full of poisonous gases. ● They can work continuously for long periods of time without a break. ● They produce exactly the same thing over and over, whereas a human would probably be less exact.	● Robots cannot think for themselves. ● They can be expensive to set up initially. ● When they break down it could take longer to replace a robot than a human. ● Human skills can be lost for ever.

Exam tip

When discussing the advantages and disadvantages of using computer control, make sure you have carefully read the question to see what the scenario is. Does the question ask about robots in car factories, looking for unexploded mines, exploring a remote planet? Then make sure your answer uses the situation given in the question.

Check your understanding

1 List **four** devices that use computer control in the home.

2 List the advantages and disadvantages of using a computer-controlled robot to spray paint cars in a factory.

3 Write a LOGO sequence that would draw a triangle with each side 100 units long.

Go online for answers

Online

Features

DTP software and word processors

Desktop publishing (**DTP**) applications are used to create publications such as newspapers or magazines, leaflets and brochures. They have more features suitable for professional publishing than standard word-processing applications which are more suited for text-based documents. A word-processing application will usually have many of the features described here, but DTP applications tend not to have so many, concentrating instead on features that allow accurate layout.

Spellchecker

A **spellchecker** automatically checks the spelling in a document. You should not rely totally on spellcheckers because there are some pitfalls to be wary of, for example

- if you type the word BEAR, but spell it wrongly as BARE, the spell checker will not flag it
- make sure the correct dictionary is being used – words can be spelled differently in American English than in UK English
- the word may be correct but not in the dictionary, such as your surname or the name of the town you live in.

Grammar checker

A **grammar checker** suggests problems with the way sentences are structured, or they can find repeated words or incorrect punctuation.

Thesaurus

A **thesaurus** can suggest alternatives for words. For example, for the word NICE, a thesaurus may suggest PLEASANT, KIND, LOVELY and other words with a similar meaning.

A **translator** will translate selected words from your word-processed document into a language of your choice.

Mail merge

Mail merge is a method of producing **personalised** letters by merging a standard letter with details of names addresses and other information from a database. For example, mail merge might be used by

- utility companies to send out bills to customers
- businesses to send circulars
- schools to send pupils their exam results.

Stages to mail merge are

1 Create a standard letter.
2 Place markers to show where details such as name and address are to be inserted.
3 Open a database of the data to be used.
4 The mail merge facility places the data from the database into each individual letter in the appropriate place.
5 Print the personalised letters.

There are many aspects to consider when producing documents.

Headers and footers

- A **header** appears at the top of every page of a document.
- A **footer** appears at the bottom of every page.

Information appearing in headers or footers might include

- the title of the document
- the name and author of the document
- page numbers automatically produced
- the date and time of printing.

Page layout

When producing a document you need to think about

- the size of the page
- the **orientation** of the page (portrait or landscape?)
- the size of the top, bottom, left and right margins
- the line spacing (single, double, or one and a half spacing).

Justification

Text can be **aligned**

- to the left
- to the right
- fully justified
- centred.

Tabulation

To make lists of data items more readable, they are often placed in columns and rows.

Using **tabs** it is easy to line up columns of data on the page.

Tables

If the lists of data are to be displayed in a grid, then a **table** should be used. The number of rows and columns can be set and column widths can be changed or cells merged to suit the data in the table.

Borders

- **Borders** can be placed around text, graphics or even pages.
- Borders can be different colours, styles and thicknesses.

Tracking and kerning

Tracking tracks any changes that are made to the document.

Kerning adjusts the spacing between characters to make the layout look visually pleasing.

Graphics

A **graphic** is an image. It might be

- a picture you have taken with a digital camera
- a picture downloaded from a website
- a piece of clipart
- a picture you have scanned.

Clipart is a ready-made graphic, often in cartoon form, that can be used to illustrate a document.

Graphics can be manipulated by

- resizing
- cropping
- rotating
- flipping (producing the mirror image).

Auto shapes

There are many different shapes already available in many packages. These are known as auto shapes.

Watermarks

A graphic or text can be placed on a **master page** where it becomes a **watermark** for the rest of the document. Everything else appearing on the document is written over the watermark which faintly shows through from the background.

File formats
Revised

When importing an image or some other sort of file from another source to include in your document you must take care which type of file it is. Most applications can recognise a variety of file types. The file type is indicated by the file extension, as in the table.

Type of file	File extension
Word file	.doc(x)
Text file	.txt
Image file	.jpg
Comma separated variable	.csv
Rich text format	.rtf

Benefits of word-processing and DTP
Revised

- High quality professional-looking publications can be created.
- Templates are available for many types of document such as letters or business cards.
- It is easy to edit the layout of a publication.
- The display is WYSIWYG (What You See Is What You Get).
- Consistency of style can be given to publications, including **house style** for businesses.
- It is possible to create more complex layouts with DTP than with a word processor.

Check your understanding
Tested

1 Name **four** different types of justification.
2 Describe the contents of a style sheet.
3 Give an example of when a mistake might not be found by a spellchecker.

Go online for answers
Online

Multimedia

Multimedia presentations

Revised ☐

A **multimedia** presentation usually involves a sequence of slides projected onto a screen.

Changing the slides may be

● controlled by the person who is explaining the topic

● automatically moved on by a timer.

A single slide may contain text, graphics, sound or video, which is why it is called multimedia.

Web pages

Revised ☐

A web page can contain many of the same features as a slide presentation. The main differences are that each 'slide' of a website is a web page and that instead of being displayed in a slide show they are accessed using the internet.

Animation

Revised ☐

The way each object appears on the slide can be selected from a number of **animation** effects.

Animation can consist of effects such as

● fly in from top (or bottom or side)

● appear randomly

● appear on a timer or on a click of a mouse button.

Slide transition

Revised ☐

The way one slide changes into another is called the **slide transition.**
This can be programmed and there are many different options to choose from, such as

● fade smoothly

● fade through black

● dissolve

● wipe-down

● wedge.

> **Exam tip**
>
> Make sure you understand the difference between animation of objects on a slide or web page and animations of page transitions. Always use the correct technical terms when answering questions in an examination.

Action buttons and hyperlinks

Revised ☐

Action buttons can be placed on a slide to perform tasks, such as

● moving to the next slide

● moving to the home slide

● opening a document

● running a movie clip

● linking to a website or another slide via a **hyperlink**.

A section of text or a graphic may be set up as a hyperlink to another slide. When the mouse button is clicked with the pointer on the hyperlink, the next slide is displayed. Hyperlinks are particularly useful on web pages where, when a hyperlink is clicked, the new page will be displayed in the browser. This is how you **navigate** between pages within a website or to other websites.

A **navigation bar** should be placed on every page of a website so that you can quickly return to the home page or move quickly between different sections.

Considering the audience

Revised

The design of a presentation or web page must take into account the purpose and the needs of the audience. A presentation to primary school pupils would use

- simple graphics
- straightforward language
- sounds to enliven the slides.

A presentation to a group of scientists might contain

- tables and/or graphs
- mathematical equations.

Not all people can see or hear as well as others, so give consideration to your use of sound, font style and font sizes and colours so you do not discriminate against those with partial sight or those who are hard of hearing. If you use images, pop-up comments can appear when a mouse hovers over them.

Some considerations that can be given to audiences are

- font sizes – these should be reasonable for most people to see from the back of a room
- font style – simple font styles are easier to read
- do not to cram too much information on a page
- make good use of contrasting colours.

Creation of a slide show

Revised

It is most important to design the content of each slide or web page carefully. Consider

- the order in which the slides are displayed
- what animation and effects to include
- the methods of slide transition
- the graphics you draw or collect
- the preparation of text, sounds and video clips.

Check your understanding

Tested

1 Describe different ways in which objects on a slide might be animated.
2 Explain the considerations you should give when designing a slide or web page for an audience.
3 Explain the term **multimedia**.

Go online for answers

Online

Data protection and copyright

Copyright law

Revised

If you have the **copyright** to something, then you are the only one allowed to copy it. Copyright law covers books, music, images, films and software.

To copy someone else's work you must have permission. You may have to pay a fee.

If you copy without permission you might be infringing the **copyright law**. In Britain this is the Copyright, Designs and Patents Act (1988).

Software piracy is the stealing or copying of software without the permission of the copyright holder.

Some companies buy site licences for software. This means they are legally allowed to copy the programs on to a given number of computers on their site.

> **Exam tip**
>
> Remember that the copyright laws cannot prevent people stealing someone else's work. However it acts as a deterrent because anyone caught doing it could be fined or imprisoned.

General Data Protection Regulation (GDPR)

Revised

Data is held about all of us on many computer systems. We have certain **rights** under the GDPR, which became law in May 2018. This law is designed to give individuals control over their personal data that is held in computer systems.

An individual who has data held about them on a computer is known as the data subject. Data subjects have the right to

● be informed if data is held about them

● consent to or object to the holding of the data

● have access to their data

● have any mistakes corrected (known as rectification)

● demand the deletion of the data

● restrict the portability of the data.

Organisations holding data about us are known as controllers and processors. They have certain obligations concerning the data. They must

● keep the data secure

● maintain a record of how the data is processed

● appoint a data protection officer.

Accidental damage to files

Revised

Data is stored on a computer system can be accidentally destroyed by the user. **Backups** can be made to help recover data accidentally destroyed.

It is important for an organisation to have a proper **back-up strategy**.

A backup of the data is an extra copy of the data. It should be

● stored somewhere different to the original copy

● made at frequent intervals

● named carefully so you know which is the most recent version.

The attribute of a file can be changed to 'read-only'. This means the file cannot be accidentally changed or deleted.

Viruses

A **virus** is a computer program which can

- copy itself from one computer file to another
- attach itself to an email so it can easily be spread
- cause damage to files stored on a computer's hard disk.

Anti-virus software can be installed on a computer to detect and remove viruses. This will protect files from possible damage by a virus, but it will need to be kept up to date because new viruses appear all the time.

Here are some precautions to take to prevent infections by a virus.

- Do not use a memory stick on a computer unless you are sure that the computer has anti-virus software installed.
- Do not open an email from a sender who you do not know.
- Never open an attachment from an unknown source.
- Do not download software from the internet unless it is from a well-known and trusted source.
- Run a virus check on a regular basis.
- Keep the virus definitions of your anti-virus software up to date.

Exam tip

It is a common mistake to write about 'virus' software in an examination. Remember it is 'anti-virus' software you need to protect your computer.

Hacking

A **hacker** is a person who gains unauthorised access to data stored on a computer.

Hackers may delete or damage data that they find.

If a hacker gets into your online bank account they could remove money from it.

Most hacking occurs because people are careless with their passwords.

Protection from hackers

- Each user should use a username and password when logging on to a system.
- Passwords need to be changed regularly.
- Obvious passwords like dates of birth or pet names should never be used.
- Never tell your password to anyone.
- Log off properly every time you have finished using a computer.

Data is in danger of being intercepted when it is being communicated over a network or over the internet. Data can be **encrypted** to prevent it being understood if it is intercepted. Encryption means the data is changed so that a hacker will not be able to understand it.

A **firewall** is software that monitors all the data going in and out of a computer and can help prevent hackers from accessing the system.

Check your understanding

1 Name the following laws.
   a) A law concerning the protection of your personal data.
   b) A law concerning illegally copying a computer game.
2 Describe **four** different ways of keeping data safe from unauthorised access.
3 Describe methods of avoiding a virus attack in your computer.

Go online for answers

Staying safe and healthy

Staying safe online

There are some dangers involved in using **social networking sites** (such as Facebook). Strangers you befriend may not be exactly as stated on their **profiles**. A person claiming to be a 15 year old girl interested in a particular band may in fact be a much older person looking for more than just an online friendship. To avoid dangers it is important that you never

- give personal data to people you have only met online
- physically meet with someone you have only met online unless you have discussed it with a responsible adult you know first.

> **Exam tip**
>
> Personal data consists of your name, email address, phone number, home address, school name and details of bank or savings accounts.

False messages

- Do not open emails or messages, files, pictures or texts from people you don't know or trust. They may contain viruses.
- Replying to a text message, for example, might put you on to a premium rate line and, before you know it, you might run up a huge bill.
- **Pharming** is a process where a website is developed by an unscrupulous person to look like another website. For example, it might pretend to be an online shop and you might buy something and enter your credit card details. You never see the goods, but you lose your money.

When online

- be on your guard
- watch out for misspelt messages – they are probably hoaxes
- look for the HTTPS symbol on the address bar – any legitimate site that needs your personal details uses it
- if an offer seems too good to be true, it usually is!

- **Phishing** is when you receive an email that pretends to come from a bank or some other source. It asks for personal and bank details. Often the email invites you to click on a link that then sends you to a fake website that looks like the real thing but its only purpose is to steal your money.
- **Spam** is email that is generalised advertising sent to anyone with an email address. It is often called **junk email**.

> **Exam tip**
>
> You may be asked in an examination to discuss appropriate steps to avoid inappropriate disclosure of personal information. A discussion involves looking at both sides, for example include both measures that are appropriate and possible to carry out, and those that are not. Never turn a discussion into a list of points. Write a conclusion at the end of your discussion.

Language

You should never use bad language online or be cruel to someone online.

If you come across bad language or get bullied (**cyber bullying**) or threatened online, report it to a responsible adult.

Webcams

Remember that webcams are looking at you and what is behind you. Make sure the webcam is switched off unless you want someone to see you. Make sure that what the other person can see does not give them clues as to where you live.

Firewalls

A firewall is hardware or software that has a set of rules about what is allowed into or out of the network. It can help protect you from unauthorised access to the network.

Health hazards

There are possible health hazards associated with using computers for long periods of time.

Hazard	Ways to reduce the risk of the hazard
Back or neck strain can be caused by using a badly positioned desk, chair or computer for long periods.	● Use an adjustable chair that is set at the correct height (forearms should be horizontal when using the computer). ● Take a five-minute break every hour or so, and walk around. ● Use a footrest.
Eye strain could be caused by using poor quality monitors, poor lighting or long hours staring at computer screens.	● Use computer screens that are set at the correct distance (an arm's length away). ● Make sure that monitors do not flicker and are not turned up too bright. ● Make sure that monitors able to swivel and are positioned at a comfortable angle. ● Place blinds over the windows to minimise glare from the sun and reflections on the screens. ● Take a five-minute break every hour or so, and look at something in the distance to exercise your eyes.
Repetitive strain injury (RSI) is the constant use of the joints in fingers, hands or wrists. It can lead to long-term pain or stiffness in the tendons.	● Use rests for wrists or arms. ● Take frequent short breaks from using a mouse or keyboard and avoid playing games for too long. ● Perform hand and wrist exercises regularly. ● Relax your grip on the mouse as tension can cause RSI. ● Position the keyboard and mouse at the correct distance and height.

Safety hazards

Revised

Computer rooms are full of electrical plugs, sockets and wires, and various pieces of equipment (some quite heavy).

Exam tip

Many candidates get muddled between health and safety. Always tackle each issue separately. Safety is more concerned with accidents that can happen suddenly whereas health issues concern more long-term problems that may occur.

Hazard	Possible prevention
Trailing wires that could be tripped over or caught, pulling heavy equipment off shelves or benches.	● Keep all wires cleared away or placed in 'cable tidies'.
Fire from overheating of plugs if too many are placed in one socket, or from overheating of equipment if ventilation grilles are covered.	● Regularly inspect plugs and sockets, and make sure they are not overloaded. ● Keep equipment free from clutter. ● Fire extinguishers must be of the powder or carbon dioxide type.
Electrocution from bare or worn wires, or badly wired plugs.	● Plugs and wires should be regularly inspected and wiring should be carried out by a qualified person.
Unsecured equipment, such as monitors or large speakers, balanced on shelves and not properly secured may fall and injure someone.	● Make sure shelves are firmly fixed and the equipment is secure on them.
Food and drink should not be used near a computer. Crumbs of food that enter the keyboard can cause sticking keys and disease. Any liquid spilt on electrical equipment could cause electric shocks.	● Never have food or drink near a computer. ● Never have a source of water in a room with a computer. ● Fire extinguishers must be of the powder or carbon dioxide type.
Water spilled onto electrical wires or equipment can cause electrocutions and damage the equipment.	

Check your understanding

Tested

1 a) List **three** items of personal data you might be asked for online.

  b) Explain why you should not believe every image you see online.

  c) List the dangers that may be found in emails or text messages.

2 List **three** health hazards in the computer room and describe how they could be prevented.

3 List **four** safety hazards in the computer room and describe how they could be prevented.

4 What is the difference between health and safety?

Go online for answers

Online

Future developments

Emerging technologies

Revised

Humans are always inventing new things and modifying old ones to make them better. Every day new discoveries are made in all branches of science, many of these directly related to ICT or using ICT to aid the discovery. Microprocessors are becoming smaller and faster, meaning that more and more processing power can be packed into ever smaller spaces and require less power to work.

A direct result of this is that materials are being produced with processors incorporated into the material itself, which may lead to

↑ **New gadgets**

- fabrics that can change colour or respond to the surroundings like a chameleon
- materials that can predict their own destruction
- tiny engines that can enter the blood stream and help fight infection
- clothing that has a mobile phone or personal organiser built into it.

You can imagine many more applications and just looking in the paper or watching television will bring many more new ideas to your attention.

Our daily lives are likely to be changed and improved and just a few ideas of how emerging technologies may affect us in the home, at school and in the environment are mentioned below.

Emerging technologies in the home

Revised

- Walls that glow, replacing electric lights.
- Windows that darken as night falls.
- Door locks with no keys, but that recognise those that live in the house.
- Surveillance systems that allow us to watch our house using a mobile phone or computer even when on holiday.
- Devices that feed the pets or control heating or lighting automatically.
- Televisions and computers becoming one single device, and possibly forming one or more walls of your sitting room.
- 3D television
- Virtual reality computer games that give 'whole body' experiences.

Emerging technologies in the home	
Advantages	**Disadvantages**
• Houses become more efficient and cheaper to run. • Homes become more comfortable to live in. • Cleaning is done automatically.	• Humans depend on machines too much and forget how to think for themselves. • Humans become lazy. • Too much surveillance means we lose all our privacy.

Emerging technologies in the school

- Biometric data might be used for registration, such as retina scanning as you enter and leave school.
- Using electronic pads instead of books to both read and write your answers.
- Speaking your answers to a computer instead of writing anything down.
- Replacing teachers or even schools with computers that you access from home.
- School dinners that are dispensed according to your vitamin and calorie requirements on the day.
- Learning helmets that automatically shape your brains to understand the latest work.
- Virtual reality experiences in the classroom to make lessons more exciting.

Emerging technologies in the school	
Advantages	**Disadvantages**
• Leaning is more exciting. • You learn more and do not forget anything. • Examinations become a thing of the past.	• Learning becomes a passive activity and so becomes boring. • With no schools there is little chance to socialise. • Teachers and other people employed to run a school lose their jobs.

Emerging technologies in the environment

- Smart meters in houses mean more efficient use of electricity, oil, gas and water.
- Electric cars give off lower emissions than petrol or diesel powered cars.
- Personal computers, worn like a bracelet or necklace, or even an earring, constantly monitor our carbon emissions and suggest alternative actions.
- ICT devices become organic rather than inorganic, so less dangerous metals will pollute the world when they are thrown away.

Exam tip

In any discussion you should try to write about the advantages and disadvantages and also to expand some of the points you make to show the consequences of that point.

Emerging technologies in the environment	
Advantages	**Disadvantages**
• The world becomes a cleaner and less dangerous place. • We become more aware of our effect on the environment and so make an effort to be 'greener' because of various sensors and meters. • ICT devices are made with recycling in mind making less throw-away waste.	• The world becomes more polluted with the ceaseless need to produce more, and replace old, ICT devices. • If, for some reason, something goes wrong, ICT controlled factories or nuclear power stations can lead to environmental disasters such as at the Chernobyl nuclear facility in the Ukraine.

Check your understanding

1 Discuss the advantages and disadvantages of studying from home using a computer link, rather than going to school.

2 Discuss ways in which ICT developments might affect the way we view films in the cinema.

3 Discuss the impact of emerging technologies on peoples' daily life at home.

Go online for answers

Online

Ensuring data quality

Encoding data Revised

Data can be **encoded**. This simplifies the way that data is represented.

A very simple example could be M for Male or F for Female

The benefits of encoding data are that

- less computer memory is used
- it is faster to enter the data once you know the codes
- fewer errors are made when entering the data
- validation of the data is easier because of the fixed set of codes.

Speed of access to data Revised

The time taken for a computer to find an item of data is known as the **speed of access**.

Data can be retrieved almost instantly from a computer storage device.

It is faster to search a database for a customer's telephone number than to use **manual** methods such as looking through a phone book.

The access time for **Random Access Memory (RAM)** is measured in **nanoseconds**.

The access time for hard drives and other secondary storage is measured in **milliseconds**.

↑ **Speed of access is the time taken from the time the request for data is made to the time the data is received**

Exam tip

One nanosecond is one billionth of a second. One millisecond is one thousandth of a second. Retrieving data from the **Immediate Access Store (IAS)** (e.g. RAM) is thousands of times faster than retrieving it from a **secondary storage device** such as a hard drive.

Using ICT for storing data	
Advantages	**Disadvantages**
• Need less storage space than using sheets of paper, record cards or filing cabinets. • Data can be stored more securely. • Data can be **encrypted** so that, if it gets into the hands of unauthorised people, they will not be able to understand or use it. • Data can be accessed very quickly. • Back-up copies can be created easily and stored in another location. • Data can be edited easily. • Data can be transmitted very quickly to another device.	• Cost of equipment can be high. • Specialist staff or training of current staff may be needed to work the equipment. • Viruses or hackers may damage the data. • Equipment failure may destroy data.

Usefulness of data Revised

Data is only useful if it is valid, sensible and up to date.

- Data **validation** is used to make sure that the data being entered is sensible (see pages 6–7).
- Data **verification** is used to ensure that the data being entered has been entered correctly.

Verification

Data can be

- copied from one medium to another (**transcribed**)
- sent from one computer medium to another (**transmitted**).

Verification checks are needed to make sure the data received is the same as the data that was sent.

These errors may be **transcription errors**.

- **Omission** – leaving out data out.
- **Transposition** – for example, typing 1324 instead of 1234.
- **Spelling mistakes** – for example, typing Davies instead of Davis.

They may be **transmission errors** caused by the **corruption** of data by electrical interference.

Methods of verification

- A person compares the source data and the transcribed data by eye. This is known as a **visual check**.
- **Double keying** is when the data is entered twice, usually by two different people and a computer compares the two versions. If they are identical, the computer will accept the data. If there are differences, an error message will be given.
- A **parity check** can be made on transmitted data. When data is transmitted it is transmitted as a series of **binary** numbers. Each binary number is a set of 0s and 1s. A single 0 or 1 is known as a bit.
  A **parity bit** is an extra bit that is added to the end of each binary number.
  - In an **even parity** system, the total number of 1s (including the parity bit) in a binary number is even.
  - In an **odd parity** system, the total number of 1s (including the parity bit) in a binary number is odd.

If a character in the data is represented by seven bits, then the parity bit can be the eighth bit.

In an even parity system 0101011 has four 1s.

This is an even number of 1s, so a parity bit of 0 is added to keep the number of 1s even. 01010110 will be transmitted.

> **Exam tip**
>
> Do not confuse a visual check with proofreading. In proofreading a document is checked for spelling and grammar. A visual check is a comparison between two documents. A visual check or verification ignores spelling and grammar.

Validation

Data **validation** is used to check that data is sensible and that it obeys certain rules.

Validation checks have already been mentioned on pages 6–7. These are range checks, presence checks, format checks and check digits.

A **batch total** is a number calculated at the start of the transmission of a batch of data. At the end of the transmission the calculation is done again and the newly calculated batch total compared with the transmitted batch total. A difference will mean an error in transmission.

A **hash total** is a batch total that has no meaning. For example, it may be the sum of people's telephone numbers or the sum of account numbers.

Check your understanding

1 Decide whether the following (correct) items of data are even or odd parity.

   a) 10111100   **b)** 11111111   **c)** 00011000

2 Name **six** different types of validation check.

3 Name **two** different types of verification.

Go online for answers

Using data logging and control

ICT and control

ICT can be used to **control** and **monitor** areas of everyday living. Measurements from **sensors** provide the input for a control process. Sensors measure quantities such as

● temperature

● light

● sound

● weight

● stress

● movement.

A computer processor will receive the inputs from the sensors. A **control program** in the processor analyses the data input and sends signals to **actuators** that control a motor, switch, tap or other device.

A **feedback system** is a control system where the output actions affect the input data, which affects the output actions, which affect the input data and so on.

> ### Exam tip
> Be careful with your spelling. There is a difference between a computer program and a TV or theatre programme. Using the correct spelling gives your work more credibility.

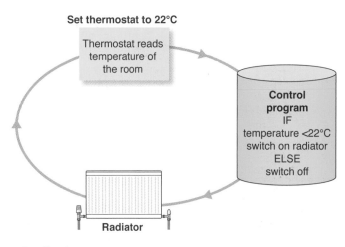

Set thermostat to 22°C

Thermostat reads temperature of the room

Control program
IF temperature <22°C switch on radiator ELSE switch off

Radiator

↑Feedback system

Examples of control systems

Automatic door

1 Start

2 Person approaches door

3 Sensor detects person

4 Actuator opens door

5 Sensors detect no person

6 Actuator closes door

7 Back to the start

Greenhouse control system

1 Start

2 Sensors detect humidity, light, temperature

3 Control program examines inputs and sends signals to actuators

4 Actuators switch on/off heaters/sprinklers, open/close blinds/windows

5 Back to start

Traffic control system

1 Start

2 Car approaches light

3 Sensor detects car

4 Control program checks other inputs from the system, before sending signal to actuator

5 Actuator switches on green light

6 Sensors detect no car

7 Actuator switches on red light

8 Back to start

Car parking systems

1 Start

2 Car approaches barrier

3 Sensor detects car arriving

4 Control program checks if car park is full. If not, sends signal to actuator. Adds 1 car to total in car park

5 Actuator lifts barrier

6 Sensor detects car leaving

7 Control program checks driver has paid. Sends signal to actuator. Deducts 1 car from total in car park

8 Actuator lifts barrier

9 Back to start

Simulation

A computer **simulation** is a model of a real system. Aircraft pilots train on a **flight simulator**. Drivers of cars and lorries can train on a **driving simulator**.

A flight simulator will look and feel exactly like flying a real aeroplane. Sensors pick up the movements of the controls as the pilot moves them and actuators will cause the model to move just like a real plane. It is cheaper and less dangerous to train pilots this way than to use a real plane. Different weather conditions such as strong winds can be simulated to allow pilots to practise flying in those conditions.

Computer control systems	
Advantages	**Disadvantages**
● Changing circumstances are monitored more frequently than a human can manage. ● Computers do not get tired or ill or take holidays. ● They will never go on strike. ● Every job is done with exactly the same precision. ● The computer will only do what it is programmed to do, so there are no surprises.	● The computer can only do what it was programmed to do so cannot adapt to changes easily. ● If there is a mistake in the programming this will be repeated endlessly until spotted.

Data logging

Computer data logging systems	
Advantages	**Disadvantages**
Readings can be ● more accurate than those taken by a human ● taken in dangerous or hazardous places ● taken at very short intervals ● read 24 hours a day, seven days a week without a break ● error free (humans make mistakes).	● Computers cannot easily respond to changing circumstances. ● Data loggers will only log what they are programmed to log.

Check your understanding

1 Give **three** areas of everyday living where a feedback cycle is used.

2 Use these words to complete the sentences below.

close   sensor   actuator   processor

In a greenhouse a _____ detects the temperature of the air. If it is too hot in the greenhouse a _____ will send signals to an _____ that will operate a motor to open the window. If it is too cold a motor will _____ the window and if necessary switch on a heater.

3 What are the advantageous of using ICT to measure the temperature, rainfall and wind speed at regular intervals on a remote uninhabited island to help with weather forecasting?

4 Look at the Control Systems examples on page 53. Write down a similar sequence for

   a) A car parking system   **b)** A traffic control system

Go online for answers

Online ☐

Data compression and file types

File storage

Revised

When files are stored on a storage device they have to be given a name.

Each file is also given a **file extension**. The purpose of the file extension is so that the user and the computer can tell, at a glance

● what type of data it is

● which applications package will open that file.

The details recorded when the file is saved will also include the size of the file, the date and time it was

2010-2011 summary.xlsx	16/02/2011 19:54	Microsoft Office Excel 2007 Workbook	12 KB
2011 Quote Summary.pdf	17/01/2011 08:00	Adobe Acrobat Document	101 KB
Chris work experience.docx	12/01/2011 09:19	Word 2007 Document	12 KB
Christmas cards.accdb	06/02/2011 09:53	Microsoft Office Access 2007 Database	576 KB

↑ **File extensions**

saved and the application it can be opened with. The extensions shown above are

● .docx – a Word file for Office 2007 or 2016

● .xlsx – an Excel file for Office 2007 or 2016

● .pdf – a Portable Document Format file

● .accdb – an Access database for Office 2007

> **Exam tip**
>
> A dot (.) should never be used in a filename to save a file because anything after the dot will be considered to be the file extension.

Data compression

Revised

There are problems associated with saving data.

● Backing storage devices have limited capacity, and large files will fill up the available storage space quickly.

● Large files will also take longer to load than smaller ones.

● If data is transmitted across a network, small files will reach their destination more quickly than larger ones.

We can use **data compression** to help overcome problems with saving large files. Files can be **compressed** to make them smaller when stored or sent over a network, but they will need to be **de-compressed** before they can be used.

Data compression	
Advantages	**Disadvantages**
Smaller file size, so ● files will take up less storage space when saved on hard disk or other storage media ● files will reach their destination more quickly when sent over a network or up/downloaded over the internet.	● Precision can be lost. ● It is not always possible to return to the uncompressed state.

Saving sound files

Revised

Sounds can be saved using

● **.wav** (wave) files, but this type of file is not compressed. The .wav file gives maximum quality and takes up a lot of space.

● **.wma** (Windows Media Audio) files can be compressed without loss of quality with some versions.

- **.mp3** (Moving Pictures Expert Group) files are also used to compress sound and are the standard in personal listening devices. Sound files with low bit rates (measured in kilobits per second) will be poorer in quality than those with higher bit rates.

Saving graphics files
Revised

Images can be saved using a number of formats.

- **.bmp** files are made up of thousands of pixels known as **bitmaps**. Each pixel is a dot that has a position and a colour recorded. The larger the image the more dots are needed to maintain quality of the image. This can make an original image file very large indeed. This means that transmitting pictures from a mobile camera or downloading pictures from a website could take a long time.

Bitmap graphic files can be compressed into other formats. Some detail may be lost, but it is usually not noticeable to the human eye. Other formats include

- **.jpeg** (Joint Photographic Expert Group) which can allow 10:1 compression with little loss of quality.
- **.gif** (Graphics Interchange Format) only uses 256 colours so is not suitable for images with continuous colours such as high quality digital photos.
- **.tiff** (Tagged Image File Format) often used in desktop publishing.
- **.eps** (Encapsulated PostScript) used for PostScript publications but provides a preview of the image and more detailed instructions for a printer.
- **.cgm** (Computer Graphics Metafile) contains instructions of how to reconstruct the image using mathematics.
- **.png** (Portable Network Graphics) made to improve on the .gif format.

> **Exam tip**
> Remember the file type is indicated by the file extension.

Saving video files
Revised

Video files can be compressed by converting them into files that compare one frame with the next and only sending data about the changes between them. (The standard format for compressed video files is MPEG **.mp4**.)

Saving folders
Revised

Groups of files can be saved as a single compressed file, but it will need to be de-compressed before the files can be used. One method of compressing files is to **zip** them (the file extension used is **.zip**).

Check your understanding
Tested

1 Choose a suitable file type by completing the table below.

Activity	File type
Recording a song to play on an iPod	
Saving a video	
Sending a photo to someone using your mobile	
Compressing a folder of files	

2 Explain why data compression is needed.

3 List the advantages and disadvantages of data compression.

Go online for answers
Online

Going online

Web software

Revised

You need software such as Microsoft Internet Explorer or Google® Chrome to retrieve information from the World Wide Web. It lets you move from website to website, or web page to web page. These applications are known as **web browsers**.

A web browser searches for the website using the site's internet address known as the **Uniform Resource Locator** (**URL**).

A URL begins with the type of internet resource that is being used so that the browser can tell what **protocol** is being used. For example

- **http** – hypertext transfer protocol
- **https** – hypertext transfer protocol over Secure Socket Layer (SSL) (which means the data is encrypted)
- **ftp** – file transfer protocol used for downloading files over the internet.

After the type of resource, the URL consists of a unique address such as www.bbc.co.uk

Browsing

Revised

You need to use **key words** to search websites that contain the information you want. These are a combination of words that should appear in the web pages you are searching for. A web browser allows you to make these **keyword searches**. Use keywords carefully. A search for a map to the Science Museum in London produces the following combinations.

Key word	Hits
Science Museum	8 370 000
"Science Museum"	3 000 000
"Science Museum London"	173 000
"Map of Science Museum London"	2

> **Exam tip**
>
> You can spot a link on a web page because it is usually underlined and a different colour to the surrounding text. The cursor changes to a pointing finger when it passes over a link.

A browser will let you store links to favourite pages. A link is a URL, but the browser will let you give the link a name to make it easier to remember. Various **menus** allow the user to choose options for the way in which the browser displays information and its appearance.

When you have found a web page you can search that page. Many websites have their own dedicated search facility or you can use the browser's 'find on this page' facility.

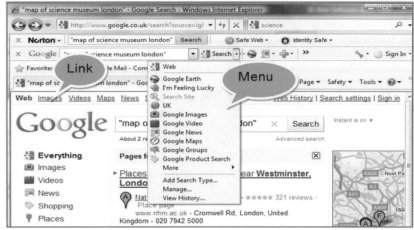

↑ Web browser features

Analysing web pages

Not all web pages are useful. When choosing a web page consider the following.

- Does the website provide exactly the information you are looking for? In other words does it meet the **original objective**?
- Is it appropriate for the **target audience**? For example, some web pages are for children, others for adults.
- Does it contain **accurate information**? Any information taken from web pages should be cross-referenced to make sure that it is correct.
- Does it provide the **right information**? If you are searching for the Science Museum in London have you found London, England? There are other towns called London in the world.
- Is the information **up to date**? You can often tell by looking at the bottom of the page to see when it was last updated.
- Is the page **unbiased**? Not all websites tell the truth and many websites provide a one-sided view rather than a balanced one.

Comparing websites

When comparing websites look for the

- **house style** – it should be possible to identify a website from any of its pages. Pages should have similar colour schemes, fonts, layouts and logos.
- **audience** – is the website aimed at adults or children, beginners or experts, men or women?
- **size** – most good websites have a site map from which it is possible to check the number of pages and the way the site is organised
- **techniques used** – look for the use of colour, pictures, sound, interesting hot spots, buttons, roll-overs, forms, searches and other features used.

Interactive features of websites

An **interactive** feature is where there is a 'conversation' between the user and the computer. Often what the user inputs will affect the output. Some interactive features are

- **online forms** – if a user types in a postcode, the form automatically supplies the address
- **email** – 'contact us' options where an email can be sent to the website
- **games** – feedback appears on the screen as a game is played in the form of scores and progress in the game
- **quizzes** – you are told whether you are right or wrong as you complete the questions
- **questionnaires** – offer choices and different pathways through the questionnaire based on answers already given.

Check your understanding

1 What do the following letters stand for?
   a) URL   **b)** HTTP   **c)** FTP
2 List **four** things you should look for on a website.
3 List **four** things you should consider when comparing websites.

Go online for answers

Creating websites

Creating web pages

Revised

All pages of a website should look similar so that the user can learn to use the website quickly and each page is instantly recognisable as belonging to the same website. This is achieved by using a **master page** which contains the general features of all the pages including

- background colour
- position of buttons
- house style logos
- font style and colours

A master page acts as a **template**. A template

- makes creating a new web page faster because the styles are already set
- makes it possible for a person unfamiliar with the website to produce a web page that has the same style as other pages.

Every website should have a **home page** that

- is the starting point for the web site
- contains buttons/links/hotpots/menus to get to other web pages on the website
- is the web page that the URL of the website finds.

It has been found that a triangular area in the upper-left corner of the screen is where people look first. This is known as the **golden triangle** of the web page. Essential information about the page should be placed there.

Site navigation is the term for exploring the web pages of a website.

A good website design will include

- a **home button** featured on every web page
- a menu on each web page of the various main areas of the website
- consistent placement of important buttons and links on every web page.

There are various **navigation tools** that can be used on the web pages.

- **Hyperlinks** are used to jump to another web page on another website. The hyperlink contains the address. The position of the link on the web page is known as an **anchor**.

- **Graphical hyperlinks** are pictures (photos, clipart, etc.) that are also hyperlinks.

- **Hotspots** are used to give more information about an area on the web page. This is activated by moving the cursor over the hot spot area or clicking on it. **Rollover buttons** are areas of the screen that change when a cursor is moved over that area.

- **Polygon links** are areas on the screen, such as an image, that have a number of different links depending where on the image you click. For example, an image of a map of the world might give the population of a country when you click on that country.

Other web page features include

- **back** and **forward buttons**
- a **refresh button** to reload or update the current resource
- **navigation bars** that contain buttons or links to other areas of the web site
- **banners** which are rectangular boxes on a web page containing text, images or animations – a **leader board** is a type of banner advertisement placed across the top of a web page

> **Exam tip**
>
> House style is the way in which web pages are designed to be recognisable as belonging to a particular website. It makes the pages consistent. Never say that house style makes the pages look professional.

↑ **Some web browser icons**

- **web icons** which are visual representations understood by everyone, such as a shopping trolley for purchasing items
- **plugins**, which are software components that are ready-built to add to to a website. They can enable foreign alphabets, allow access to proprietary software and display their pages, or allow access to social media, among other things.

Creating a website

Revised

A **website** could comprise one or many **web pages**.

A **web server** is the computer linked to the internet that will hold the web pages. It is known as the **host**. An **Internet Protocol** (**IP**) address is the actual address of the web server.

To create a website you need to

- choose your topic
- plan the different web pages
- decide how the web pages are to be linked by creating a **structure diagram**
- choose a theme for colours, font size and style

- choose a **domain name** (which must be unique)
- create your web pages and test that all the links work
- find a host and upload the website to the host computer.

Issues with the hosting of websites

Revised

When selecting a host for a website, you need to consider the following.

- The **security** of the web server.
- **Updates** to web pages need to be made regularly.
- Internal and external **links** should be tested regularly.
- Make sure your data is still **reliable**.
- Avoid breaking **copyright** regulations.
- Keep the website **unbiased**.
- Choose a host where the **speed of response** is fast and the upload speeds are good.
- **Optimise** the graphics before they are placed on the website so they will take up less memory space and can be downloaded faster.
- Use **thumbnails** hyperlinked to a full sized image.

Colours

Revised

Colours used on web pages use the **RGB system** because all colours can be made from a combination of red, green and blue. Computers use numbers to work out which colour to use on each pixel. These numbers can be in decimal (the base ten numbers we use every day) or hexadecimal (base 16 numbers).

Colour	Decimal (RGB)	Hexadecimal
White	255,255,255	FFFFFF
Blue	0, 0, 255	0000FF
Yellow	255,255,0	FFFF00

Check your understanding

Tested

1 Describe the contents of a master page for a website.
2 a) Describe the term **site navigation**. b) Name **four** aids to site navigation.
3 Using the RGB system, what hexadecimal number is used for
   a) green   b) magenta (a mixture of red and blue)?

Go online for answers

Online

Creating slide presentations

Presentation software

Presentation software, such as Microsoft PowerPoint, is used to produce a set of slides. Each slide is capable of containing text, images, sound and video. Various effects can be included to vary the way that the information appears on the screen. This is known as **slide animation**.

Design templates

A **master slide** facility allows the user to set

- the backgrounds to the slides
- the fonts used as heading and body font
- the colour scheme
- other items, such as logos or images, that will appear on every slide.

Presentation software packages often provide **templates** already set up for such things as quizzes, photo albums and calendars.

By using templates, a presentation can also project a **house style**.

> **Exam tip**
> House style can also be referred to as corporate style.

Animation effects

Any part of a presentation, such as text, graphics or charts, can be animated. Animation is carried out to emphasise important points by attracting the attention of the audience.

Animation can be automatic or activated by clicking a mouse button.

Animation effects available are

- bulleted lists appear one bullet at a time
- bullets can 'fly in' from the left or right
- text can appear by the letter, word or paragraph
- text or objects can be dimmed or change colour.

Transitions and timings

The effect applied as one presentation slide changes to another slide is called the **slide transition**.

A presentation can be set to run **automatically** (with no human intervention) or **manually** (with slides **transitioning** from one to another on a mouse click or equivalent). Automatic presentation is often set to run continuously in a loop. For example, it is useful

- to describe an exhibit in a museum or shop window
- to show the achievements made by the school during the year
- when a presenter is not available.

Some disadvantages of automatic presentation are

- the presentation might move too slowly (or quickly) for the audience
- it might break down and only the audience notices
- it is not possible to ask questions because there is no-one to ask.

Manual presentation	
Advantages	**Disadvantage**
• The presenter can answer questions. • The presenter can pause the presentation at a slide (to expand on a point being made, for example).	• The presenter has to be present.

Presentation features

Revised

Many features can appear in presentations and these are summarised in the table below.

Feature	Description
Text	Words, characters or numbers.
Image	A picture or cartoon.
Sound	A clip of music, voice or some other sound, such as applause, animal noises, car starting up.
Video	A clip of moving pictures.
Animation	Movement of the text or other objects on the page.
Slide transition	Special effects that happen when one slide changes to another such as fade, wipe, explode, fly-in. The timing of the animations can be preset or they can be operated by a click of a mouse button.
Hyperlink	A link that, when clicked, will move to another part of the presentation or to somewhere outside the presentation.
Hotspot	An area on the screen that will respond to a click of the mouse button.
Button	A feature, like a hotspot, that will respond to a mouse button click.
Navigation bookmarks	Links that are saved so that you can jump back to them at any time. If the presentation is linked to the internet, they can be URLs to external slides or pages.

Narration and speaker notes

Revised

During manual transition the presenter can use **speaker notes** which show on the presenter's screen, but the audience cannot see them. This keeps the notes with the slides rather than having separate documents.

Printing formats

Revised

There are various print options such as

- individual slides
- several slides to a page
- printout with notes
- outline view
- delegate's copy with area to make notes.

Presentation software	
Advantages	**Disadvantages**
● Easy to standardise slides using templates. ● Slides can be saved to disk or memory stick. ● Slides are easy to edit. ● Order of slides can be changed easily. ● Slides cannot be dropped and become out of order. ● Slides can include special effects such as sound, video, animation. ● Presentations can be set to run automatically.	● Relies on a computer. ● Training needed to use the computer. ● Computers can sometimes be unreliable and crash or not connect to the projector. ● If there is no computer or projector at a venue where the presentation is to be held then expensive and heavy equipment needs to be carried there. ● It is difficult to annotate the slides during a presentation.

Check your understanding

Tested

1 Describe slide animation.

2 Describe slide transition.

3 State the advantages and disadvantages of using presentation software.

Go online for answers

Online

Multimedia components

Hardware

Revised ☐

The term **multimedia** is used when text, sound, still images, animation and video are combined together to give

- a production, such as a slide show presentation
- an interactive production, such as a computer game, quiz, search or questionnaire.

Multimedia is also used to describe the hardware used to produce and present the multimedia productions.

Multimedia hardware

Revised ☐

For a multimedia system you need

- a good sized, **high resolution** screen
- a mouse, game pad or tracker ball
- good quality speakers
- a fast processor
- a high specification graphics card
- a large hard drive
- a DVD or Blu-ray drive.

Other hardware devices needed might be

- touch sensitive input devices, such as touch pads
- motion-sensing input devices, such as sensors that can detect movement
- force-sensing input devices, such as sensors able to detect a force applied to them; some digital bathroom or kitchen scales use force sensors
- a microphone, if you wish to input voice, music and other sounds.

Output devices for multimedia systems

Revised ☐

- Screen – the size of a screen is measured by an imaginary line drawn diagonally across the screen from corner to corner. A high resolution screen is one with a high number of pixels per cm^2. (See page 56 for more details of resolution.)
- Speakers – for a good multimedia system you need at least two speakers to give stereo effects, many also include a larger speaker to give bass effects.

Input devices for multimedia systems

Revised ☐

- Mouse, game pad or tracker ball to control movements on the screen, activate commands and select from menus.
- Microphone to communicate with others in interactive games or to give voice activated commands.
- Touch-sensitive screens or touch pads.
- Graphics tablet – this is a board covered by a touch-sensitive membrane that can be used to **digitise** anything drawn on it. A **stylus** is used to draw. Graphics tablets can also be called **concept keyboards** and can be used to interact with the computer by touching different parts of the tablet.

Exam tip

A computer processes data when it is in binary form. The process of turning data into binary digits is known as digitising data.

Methods of image capture

For images to be used in multimedia systems they must be **captured** and digitised. There are several ways of capturing images.

- A **scanner** can digitise graphics that are printed or drawn on paper.
- A **digital camera** can capture still images.
- A **video camera** can capture moving images.
- **Webcams** are found built into many laptops.
- **High dynamic range (HDR)** cameras, often found in mobile phones, capture greater detail in the dark and light parts of a photo.

With all image capturing devices, the higher the resolution, the better the quality of the image.

Multiple cameras is a method used in film-making where several cameras are filming at once, often ranged around the subject, some taking close-ups.

3D imaging is a method whereby the human brain is tricked into thinking that it is looking at an image in three dimensions. This effect is achieved by taking two images of the same scene from different angles and merging them to create a single image.

Musical Instrument Digital Interface

Musical Instrument Digital Interface (**MIDI**) is a method by which musical instruments can act as input devices to the computer. Advantages of MIDI are that

- different instruments can play different tracks that can be recorded on hard drive and then **mixed** and the tracks played together
- software can produce printed music directly from the music played to aid composing
- each individual track can be edited before the final result, for comparative volume and tone.

Software and memory requirements for multimedia

Data input to a computer first enters the **immediate access store** (**IAS**) which is a temporary storage area. It is then stored (saved) to a backing store such as a hard disk. IAS is sometimes called **internal memory**.

A backing store can take the form of **physical media**, such as hard drives or flash memory cards, or remote media such as cloud memory, accessed over the internet and based in remote servers.

Specialist software can be used for

- digital photographic editing
- movie making
- animation
- creating music
- capturing and editing sound.

> **Exam tip**
>
> IAS, such as RAM, is **volatile** so it loses its contents when power is switched off. To save data permanently, data should be saved to backing storage such as a hard drive or DVD.

Check your understanding

1 Define multimedia.
2 List the input devices used in multimedia systems.
3 List the output devices used in multimedia systems.

Go online for answers

Multimedia software

Multimedia components

Multimedia software	
Advantages	**Disadvantages**
• Much multimedia software is standardised so it works on most computers. • Results can be saved to disk or memory stick for easy portability. • It is easy to send multimedia productions by email or view over the internet. • Special effects such as sound, video and animation increase audience interest. • There are pre-made templates designs to choose from for slide show and home movie production.	• It relies on a computer. • Someone must be trained to use the computer. • Computers can sometimes be unreliable and crash. • Expensive and heavy equipment might need to be carried around and could get stolen.

Techniques for storing text, images, sound and video

Text

- is generally stored as a document using file types such as **.doc** or **.docx** (indicating the package to be used to read the file)

- can be stored as **.txt**, which is a generic format and can be read by almost any application capable of reading text

- file sizes are generally small

- is saved using **American Standard Code for Information Interchange** (**ASCII**) – each character is changed to a number.

Images

- Images can be saved as a bitmap **.bmp** file where each pixel of the image is recorded.

- Good quality images generally make very large files so they often need to be compressed using file types such as **.jpg** or **.gif** formats.

Sound

- Sound can be stored as an **analogue** file where a physical change records the music such as using the grooves of old-fashioned records.

- The sound waves can be **digitised** so all the sounds are represented in uncompressed binary form such as **.wav**.

- Compressed sound files such as **.mp3** are popular because they are quicker to transmit and take up less storage space than uncompressed files.

Video

- Videos consist of many **frames** each of which can be saved making a large file.

- Compressed video files record only the changes between the frames as in **.mpg** files.

Storing compressed multimedia files	
Advantages	**Disadvantages**
● Less storage space is used so more data can be recorded on a given medium. ● Files are smaller so transmission time over the internet will be quicker. ● Files are standardised to recognisable formats.	● Quality and detail could be lost. ● It is not always possible to de-compress a compressed file to retrieve the original.

Current developments in multimedia

Revised

Multimedia is being used in **education** to produce

● computer-based training (CBT) courses

● slide show presentations to aid classroom teaching

● automatic displays in school foyers or on speech day

● student course work

● interactive quizzes and questionnaires.

Multimedia is being used in **entertainment**

● in interactive computer games

● in creating home movies

● in slide presentations at weddings or special occasions

● to listen to music while watching the videos

● to create special effects in movies and animations

● to create art.

Multimedia is being used in **business**

● to make presentations used to introduce or sell products

● to communicate new ideas at conferences

● in advertisements on television.

Multimedia is being used in **society**

● Modern society depends on television, radio, internet and film, all of which use multimedia to communicate.

● Live news is reported from around the world with the aid of sound, text and pictures.

● Mobile phones are able to keep us in touch around the world and most are able to function with all forms of multimedia.

↑ A social networking site

Check your understanding

Tested

1 Name a file type used to compress

a) video

b) sound

c) images

2 Explain the advantages and disadvantages of using compressed files.

3 Name **four** areas where multimedia is being used.

Go online for answers

Online

Graphics

Vector and bitmap graphics

Revised

Bitmap graphics

- Made up of pixels where each pixel has a position and a colour.
- The pixels are very small and so many are placed together they fool the human eye into thinking they are connected.
- The larger the image the more dots are needed to maintain the quality.
- Bitmap images are sometimes known as **raster** images.
- Bitmaps are best used for photographs and images with subtle shading because vector graphics cannot produce the huge number of colours available to a bitmap.

Vector graphics

- Consist of equations that describe the relative distance of a point from the point of origin.
- Components are also described by length, thickness and colour.

Advantages of vector graphics over bit mapped graphics

- Vector drawings can be enlarged to any size without any loss in quality. Bitmaps become **pixelated** when enlarged.
- Vector graphics are ideal for company logos, large banners, posters and other images that may need to be greatly enlarged.
- Vector image file sizes are smaller than bitmaps taking up less storage space.
- Vector graphic file sizes are smaller so they are faster to load than bitmaps.

 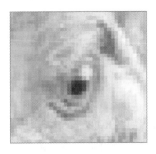

↑ **Enlargement of a bitmap graphic shows pixelation**

Pixels

Revised

A pixel is a dot of colour or **picture element** of a graphic that is a particular colour.

The **resolution** of a picture is measured in pixels. An image described as a 640 × 480 image is 640 pixels wide and 480 pixels high.

The resolution of an image is described by how many **pixels per square inch (ppi)** are capable of being shown on the monitor. The more pixels per square inch the greater the **density** of dots so the higher the quality of the picture.

A high density screen will be clearer than a low density one.

The resolution of printers is often called **dots per inch** (**dpi**) rather than ppi.

Sizing of images

Revised

When using a digital camera you can set the resolution of the images using the camera software.

- A low resolution allows you to store more images in a given space.
- The quality of a low resolution image will not be as good as a high resolution one.
- A high resolution image will be of good quality but the files are very large.
- If the images are going to be sent over a network or pasted into a document, then a low resolution is desirable.
- If the image is to be used artistically and perhaps printed onto an A4 or A3 sheet, then a high resolution setting would be better.

Units of measurement

Revised

If the vertical and horizontal resolutions are multiplied together and divided by one million you end up with the number of **megapixels** of the image.

For example

> Image size 3000 × 3000 pixels
>
> 3000 × 3000 = 9 000 000
>
> Dividing by 1 000 000 gives 9 megapixels

Digital camera memories are measured in **gigabytes**. One gigabyte is 1024 × 1024 × 1024 bytes of memory, or over 1000 million bytes.

Memory requirements for different backgrounds

Revised

Different backgrounds demand different amounts of memory.

For example, if you choose a small image and 'tile' it across the page, it will use far more memory than if you create just one image and use it as a background.

Images are often made of **layers**. The more layers your image has, the more memory it will use.

Check your understanding

Tested

1 Work out the resolution of an image 3000 × 1000 pixels. Give the answer in megapixels.
2 If an image from a digital camera uses 2 megabytes, approximately how many images could be stored using a 1 GByte memory card?
3 Explain the advantages of using vector graphics over bitmap graphics.

Go online for answers

Online

Creating and manipulating still images

Standard tools

Zoom

Zoom allows you to view the image on the screen larger or smaller than it first appeared. This is useful for delicate close up work such as getting rid of a spot on a photo.

Selection

The **selection** tool is really useful for choosing part of an image to work on. The selection tool lets you form a barrier from the rest of the image so that what you do inside the selected area does not affect the rest of the image.

Transforming

Images can be **transformed** from one state to another with a graphics package, such as using **rotation** and **reflection**.

Scaling and sizing

Images can be **scaled**, which means that they can be **resized** or **distorted** in some way.

Resizing means that the image is made smaller or larger but the proportions stay the same.

Scaling means the image size can be changed as a percentage of the original.

Brush settings

Most graphics packages will offer a large variety of **brush tips** and colours. The brush tip defines the shape of the trace as the brush is moved across the page.

Distortion

Distortion can add movement and interest to an image. It is possible for you to produce the effect of movement or action or just artistic interpretation using this tool.

Types of distortion might be **twirl**, **ripple** or **wave**.

Cloning

If you wish to remove a part of an image it can be changed to look like another part of the image by **cloning**. This involves using a 'magic brush' or clone tool that traces over part of the image and produces a copy of what it is copying on another part of the image. The size of the brushes can be altered to carry out fine cloning or coarse cloning.

Layering

When you draw an image, for example a logo, it can be built up from a number of layers. The order in which the layers overlap can be changed, so that something at the back can appear at the front and so on. The transparency of a layer can be changed too so that it is possible to see through the layer to what is behind it.

You can move or **toggle** between layers by using 'send to back', 'bring to front' and so on, or use the layering tools of the package to choose which layer you are working on or viewing.

Moving

Moving images from one part of a composition to another can be carried out using

- **cut and paste**, if you wish to actually remove an image from one part of the composition to another
- **copy and paste**, if you wish to preserve the original and have other copies of the image in the composition.

↑ Colour effects

Rotating

An image can be turned about an axis through a number of degrees.

Reflection

Reflection is sometimes called flipping and means producing a mirror image of something.

Colour

Most art packages provide many methods of dealing with colour. These might be

- **colour effects**
- **colour palettes**
- **colour gradients**.

↑ Colour palettes   ↑ Colour gradients

Imaging effects

Revised

When something is **transparent** it means that it is possible to see through it. The degree of transparency of an object can be changed so that it is either 100% transparent (you can see right through it to the background) or 0% transparent (you cannot see through it at all).

The opposite to transparent is **opaque**. You may sometimes see opacity referred to rather than transparency.

Composite patterning

Revised

A pattern may consist of many parts, such as in many fabric or wallpaper designs. When the whole pattern is repeated, it is known as **composite patterning**.

↑ Composite pattern

Check your understanding

Tested

1 Describe the meaning of zoom.
2 Describe **three** different ways of dealing with colour in an art package.
3 Compare rotation with reflection.

Go online for answers

Online

Use of movement

Animation

Revised ☐

Animation means making something move, for example

● making letters or words move when using presentation software

● making a cartoon image move

● making a 3D model move.

All animations are created by using many images, each one having a tiny difference from the previous one. When the images are displayed rapidly one after another it appears as if they are moving.

Persistence of vision

Cartoon films began to appear in cinemas at the start of the twentieth century. They were produced in the following way.

1 An artist drew a picture.

2 A photograph of the picture was taken.

3 The picture was altered slightly.

4 Another photo was taken.

5 And so on.

Afterwards the photos were displayed rapidly one after the other to make it seem as if the images in the pictures were moving.

The process by which the eye is fooled into thinking that still pictures are moving is known as **persistence of vision**.

1 Your eye 'clicks' on an image.

2 Your brain processes the image.

3 Your eye 'clicks' on another image.

The process happens quickly so your brain thinks that the images are a continuous process and that the images you are seeing are moving.

You are seeing what you expect to see.

The speed at which images are displayed is measured in frames per second (fps).

Your eye will perceive a smooth flow of graphics at around 100 fps. Fewer than that and the film will appear jerky or as a series of still images.

Flip books

Revised ☐

The first animations were **flip books** where the drawings on each page were slightly different from the drawings on the pages before. These are still widely produced. As you flip the pages, the pictures seem to move.

Stop motion animation

Revised ☐

Stop motion is where a series of photos of a model are taken.

1 A model is made out of plasticine or clay.

2 A photo of the model is taken.

3 A small change is made to the model.

4 Another photo is taken

5 And so on.

When you play the photos back rapidly it looks as if the model is moving.

It is possible to create animation in 2D (two dimensions) or 3D (which gives a three dimensional look to the images).

Key frame animation

Revised

Key frames are drawn by an artist. These are usually what an image looks like at the start of a sequence and what it looks like at the end.

The background would probably stay much the same.

Other artists, known as **in-betweeners** create the drawings to go between one key frame and the next. The more in-between drawings made, the smoother the cartoon will look.

Uses of animation in commercial environments

Revised

Films often include exciting scenes, such as explosions, spaceships, robots, aliens, car chases and so on. Trying to film the real scene might be far too expensive, dangerous or even impossible, so special effects are used. Special effects often involve **computer-generated imagery** (**CGI**).

Web animations are used to make web pages more interesting and eye-catching. Designers use a variety of methods including

● animated GIFs

● dynamic HTML

● Java®

● Shockwave® and Flash®.

Standard banners for web pages will often contain animated graphics. Logos are often used to create a **corporate identity** so that a person will instantly recognise the site they are looking at.

Uses of animation in learning environments

Revised

A **Virtual Learning Environment** (**VLE**) is one in which the student is not apparently confined to the classroom to study.

VLEs use

● smart boards

● the internet

● computer-based learning.

It is possible to sit in your classroom but explore the world.

Check your understanding

Tested

1 Describe persistence of vision.

2 Describe animation.

3 Describe stop motion.

Go online for answers

Online

Creating animated images

Commercial uses of animation

Animation in commerce	
Advantages	**Disadvantages**
● Interesting interactive effects can be made on websites. ● Film makers can save money, produce films more safely and create 'impossible' effects, such as bullets that turn corners. ● Successful films earn lots of money!	● Web pages can be slow to load. ● Some browsers may not be able to display the effects. ● Films become increasingly unbelievable. ● People try 'impossible' stunts at home and hurt themselves.

Planning an animation sequence

A film or cartoon sequence must be planned carefully in advance of production.

You will need to take into account

● the intended **audience** – e.g. adult, child, learned or uninformed

● the subject matter you are presenting

● the length of the sequence

● any sounds you are using.

Storyboards allow you to decide

● what is going to happen as you move through the sequence

● the order in which the events unfold

● the colour, shape and sound of each section.

Storyboards are also used to plan websites and can show the relationship of the web pages to each other.

Mood boarding is used in fashion, interior design, website planning and so on. A mood board consists of a collage or collection of colours, pictures, ideas, font types, etc. that, in a very casual way, depict the overall feel of what you are trying to do. For example, a mood board for a bedroom design advert could contain paint colours, fabrics, pictures of bedroom furniture, etc. to 'set the mood'.

Folder trees show the relationship of folders to each other. **Nested folders** are folders inside folders. Folder trees are a useful aid to designing web sites.

↑ **Folder tree**

Frame rates and looping

Each separate image of an animation is called a **frame**. The rate at which these frames are displayed is known as the **frame rate**. Some sequences of frames can be displayed over and over again to give a certain effect such as a waterfall or moving sea. This is known as **looping**.

Vector and bitmap animation

Bitmap images are made up of thousands of pixels, whereas a vector graphic has its lines defined by mathematical formulas. When using animation these differences need to be taken into account. Imagine you have a background of trees and in front of the trees a bird is flying around. The bitmap is rendered and exists as a single image but the vector graphic only exists as an equation and must be reworked every time the screen is refreshed.

Claymation and pixilation

Revised

Claymation is a method of using clay or plasticine models to create an animated sequence using the stop motion technique.

Pixilation is a method where live actors take the place of the clay models. A picture is taken, the actor moves slightly and another picture is taken and so on. Later the images of the actor are replaced by a monster or other creature.

Rotoscoping

Revised

In **rotoscoping**, the animator draws round an image of an actor, animal or other moving object frame by frame. These images can then be transferred into the animated film and changed so that, for example, an actor becomes a strange alien or a motor bike is transformed into a hover machine.

Onion skinning and tweening

Revised

Onion skinning works as follows.

1   The first key frame is placed on a light box.

2   A transparent sheet of paper, known as an **'onion skin'**, is placed over the key frame.

3   The key frame drawing is copied on to the 'onion skin' with a slight difference to it.

4   After a number of the 'onion skins', the last one should match the next key frame.

It is possible using animation software to use a process called **tweening** to create in-between frames automatically. The movement between the frames, when produced automatically, may not be exactly what you want, so the frames might need to edited or **tweaked** to get them just right.

Grouping

Revised

A **backdrop** is the background to a frame of a film or animation.

Images are often a collection of separate parts. These need to be **grouped** so that they do not become separated when the composite image is moved. The images can then be moved to different positions on the backdrop to give the effect you require.

Check your understanding

Tested

1   Name **three** different methods of producing animations.

2   What should be taken into account when planning an animation sequence?

Go online for answers

Online

Sound hardware

Storing sound

Revised

Sound can be stored in an analogue format or in a digital format (where the sound waves are **digitised**).

The digitised files might be **.wav** or **.mp3** files.

These files can then be saved on CD, DVD, hard drives or flash memories.

Sound cards

Revised

Computers have **sound cards** which process the sounds produced by the computer and send them to the speakers. The sound card has an interface that allows you to plug in a microphone and speakers, or lets you transfer sound to another device.

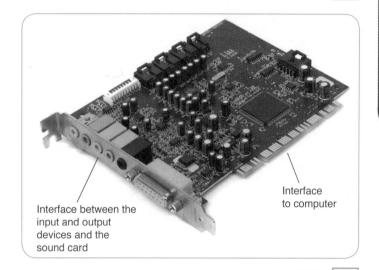

Interface between the input and output devices and the sound card

Interface to computer

Microphone

Revised

Microphones are used to input sound into a device. For example, a microphone might be used

- as an input device for people whose hands are occupied (surgeons, people driving vehicles or flying aircraft)
- as an input device for those who have a disability in their hands.

A microphone can be used as an input device to a computer, for example

- for teleconferencing
- in speech recognition systems, where the user can dictate to the computer using speech.

Most digital cameras have the ability to record sound as well as pictures when taking moving pictures.

Speakers

Revised

Speakers output sound from a device such as a computer. Different speakers have the capacity to play different frequency of sounds. The bigger the speaker, the lower the sound that it can produce.

Big heavy speakers are sometimes called **woofers** and are generally used for bass notes, whereas high frequency speakers are called **tweeters** and are used for higher frequency sounds.

Sound and music

Revised

Musical instruments can communicate with a computer using a defined standard called **Musical Instrument Digital Interface** (**MIDI**). MIDI instruments are musical instruments that can be connected to a computer. Digital signals are input to the computer as you play the instrument and these can then be stored as a data file and later processed, edited or played back through the instrument.

For example, keyboards are common MIDI instruments, and you can play a piece of music that is directly input to the computer and stored digitally. The piece can easily be edited with special software by changing the notes, tempo, dynamics and even the sound of the instrument before playing it back through the keyboard.

Other common MIDI instruments are guitars, drums and other instruments that can produce artificially produced sounds. **Sound synthesisers** are usually in the form of musical keyboards with the capability of producing or sequencing many different musical sounds.

A computer can be used to record a musical **track** playing one instrument on the synthesiser. Another track can then be played and recorded alongside the first. In this way it is possible to build up a whole 'orchestra' of musical sounds. Voice can be added if required. **Sequencers** or multi-track recording studios use software designed to help produce music using a computer. Musical scores can be written using a **notator**.

> **Exam tip**
>
> Any device with a MIDI-OUT port can control any device with a MIDI-IN port. This is because MIDI is a defined standard.

Sound wave editors

Revised

Sounds are analogue signals and are heard when a sequence of sound waves hits our ear drums. It is possible to sample and edit these waves to change the sound we hear.

Sound wave editors may be purchased, or some can be downloaded free from websites.

Downloading music

Revised

Almost all music ever recorded is available on websites. You can easily find almost any sound clip you want. However there are problems with downloading music files because they may be under copyright. This means that you should always check to see if you have permission to download the file, or you may need to pay for them. Most music files and live performances earn someone a living. By stealing their music you may be denying them a chance to provide food and care for themselves and their families.

> **Exam tip**
>
> When answering any question about downloading files over the internet, mention the possible dangers of importing a computer virus, especially if the source is not well known.

Check your understanding

Tested

1 Explain the difference between woofers and tweeters.
2 Explain why a sound card is needed in a computer.
3 What does MIDI stand for?

Go online for answers

Online

Connectivity

Networks

Revised

A **network** is when two or more computers are connected together to exchange data.

Each computer must have

- a network interface card (NIC)
- network communications software.

Once the computers are linked together they can share resources and communicate between each other.

A computer that is not linked to a network is called a **stand-alone** computer.

Local area network

Revised

A network of computers in the same building or on the same site is called a **Local Area Network** (**LAN**). LANs are generally found in homes, offices and schools. The links connect the computers using cabling or wireless.

Wide area network

Revised

A network of computers connected over a wide geographic area is called a **Wide Area Network** (**WAN**). An example of a WAN may be a business that has offices in a number of different countries around the world. The connections to computers on a WAN are made using the telephone network and satellites. The internet is an example of a WAN.

Network topology

Revised

The way in which a network is configured is called a **network topology**. You need to know about three network topologies: the **bus**, **star** and **ring** networks.

Bus network

A bus network consists of a common cable called a bus.

- Each computer is linked into the bus.
- Bus networks are the cheapest to set up.
- If one computer on the network fails the others can still carry on communicating.
- Data travels in both directions on the bus.
- The speed of data communication in a bus network is slow.

Star network

All the computers in a star network are connected to a central computer (**file server**) or a **hub**.

- The hub directs the flow of data in the network.
- Each computer has its own connection to the hub so failure of one computer will not affect the rest of the network.

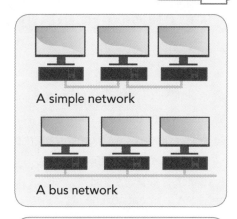

A simple network

A bus network

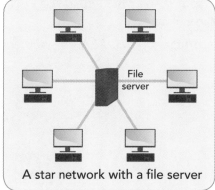

A star network with a file server

- If the hub or file server fails, then all computers will be affected.
- A star network is more expensive to install than a bus network because it uses more cable.
- It is faster and more reliable than a bus because each computer has a direct link to the hub.

Ring network

The computers in a ring network are connected to each other in a continuous loop.

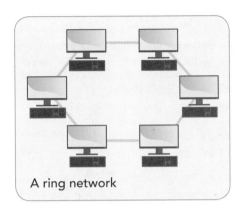

A ring network

- Computers on a ring network communicate by sending data round the loop, always in the same direction, each one passing it on to the next, until it reaches the receiving computer.
- A ring network has the problem that if one computer or cable breaks down then the whole network will be affected.

Internet and intranet

Revised

The **internet** is a network of computers across the world.

- It uses telephone lines and satellite links to communicate.
- It allows data and resources to be shared.
- Activities, such as messaging, shopping, banking, teaching and advertising, take place online.
- The coverage is world-wide and is generally unrestricted by rules.

An **intranet** is a network providing similar services to the internet.

- It is generally limited to one organisation, such as a company or school.
- There are restrictions to who can use it and what they can use on it.

The **World Wide Web** (**WWW**) is the collection of multimedia information or resources available on the internet.

Network components

Revised

A **router** is a device that

- forwards data packets along a network
- is generally located at **gateways** (where two networks connect)
- determines the best path for forwarding the packets
- communicates with other routers to work out the best route between any two workstations.

A **switch** is a device that filters data packets and forwards the packets between segments of the network.

A gateway is a system to allow a LAN to connect with a WAN, such as the internet.

A **bridge** connects a LAN to another LAN that uses the same protocol.

Packet switching

Revised

Data is moved around a network in **packets**.

Packet switching is the process by which network components check each packet, look at its address and direct it along the correct route.

Each packet consists of binary digits and contains

- **control data** (how many packets are being sent, which packet in the set it is)
- an **address** of where it is going
- the data it is delivering.

The advantages of using packets as opposed to direct wire links are

- if one packet out of a transmission fails to arrive only that one packet has to be resent
- packets from the same transmission can take different routes but all arrive at the same destination
- the transmission can reassemble at the destination because each packet contains information about how many other packets there are in the transmission and where in the transmission it fits.

Advantages and disadvantages of networks versus stand-alone computers

Revised

- A stand-alone computer is less vulnerable to virus attack and hacking, whereas a networked computer needs extra protection, such as firewalls.
- A stand-alone computer has no communication with other computers, whereas data sharing is possible in a network.
- A stand-alone computer needs its own printer, scanner and storage devices, but computers on a network can share this hardware.
- Each stand-alone computer needs its own software installed, but software can be shared over a network.
- Data entered into a stand-alone computer is only available to the user of that computer, but all data can be shared on a network.
- Stand-alone computers are not as easily controlled as network computers where a network manager can allocate permissions to users, restrict their actions or limit the amount of storage space they can use.
- If data files accessed by users on a network are stored on a file server, then it is easier to make scheduled backups than if the files are stored on several different computers.

Check your understanding

Tested

1 Name **three** different network topologies.
2 Compare stand-alone computers with networked computers.
3 Explain packet switching.

Go online for answers

Online

Point of Sale and stock control systems

Point of Sale systems

Revised

The checkout tills in large stores and supermarkets are usually linked to a computer that monitors the sale of items. The till is often called a **Point of Sale** (**POS**) terminal.

The data can be input to the POS system using

- a barcode reader/scanner
- a keypad
- electronic scales
- a magnetic stripe.

Data is output to

- a display screen
- a printer (to print the receipt, tokens and vouchers)
- a speaker (to beep as goods go through).

↑ **POS terminal**

Some supermarkets have self-service tills where you can scan your own goods.

Information from the POS terminal is sent to a computer. This information includes

- the barcode of the item
- the cashier who scanned it
- the terminal they are working at
- the time the item was scanned
- the number of items scanned
- the weight of certain items
- details of loyalty cards, coupons and special offers.

The system processes this information in **real time** and sends back information such as

- description of the item
- deductions for special offers
- number of loyalty points earned
- total of all the prices (amount to be paid)
- date and time purchase was completed.

When a customer buys an item in a shop that uses a POS terminal, the sequence of events is as follows.

1 The item being purchased is identified by reading a barcode and sometimes by typing in a code or weighing the item.

2 The data is sent to the main computer.

3 The computer looks up the item in its database and sends details, such as the description and price of the item, back to the POS terminal.

4 The description and price are displayed on a screen for the customer to see.

5 When all items have been processed, the total bill is calculated and an itemised receipt is printed for the customer.

6 The customer pays for the goods either with cash, by cheque or using a card.

All the information received is processed by the system to aid in stock control.

Stock control and order processing

Stock is the name for all the goods a business has for sale.

Stock level is the quantity of a particular item in the shop or warehouse.

Stock control is the overall management of stock levels.

Controlling the amount of stock in a shop is important for a number of reasons.

- If a shop has too many of any one item it may not be possible to sell them all.
- Some stocks, such as meat or fish, are perishable and they may go bad before they can be sold.
- Shops need to reduce wastage so they do not spend money on goods they are unable to sell.
- If the shop has too few of any item, then it may run out and anger or disappoint the customer. If the customer cannot find what they want they may not return to that shop again.
- The shop management can use the records of sales to analyse patterns of spending and make effective and productive management decisions.

Most large shops now have **automatic stock control** systems. These are designed

- to make sure no item of stock runs out
- to make sure no item is over-ordered and over-stocked (e.g. Christmas puddings still unsold in March!)
- to make sure just enough of a perishable item is stocked, so it can be sold before passing the sell-by date
- to keep track of the stock levels of all goods
- to order more goods from the suppliers if the stock level falls below the **reorder level**
- to analyse which items are selling well and which are not
- to adjust the reorder level on the basis of the analysis
- to allow for seasonal adjustment for some items.

Reports can be produced giving such information as

- total sales figures
- a list of the best selling items
- all items that need reordering
- items that have not sold well.

> **Exam tip**
>
> Remember the distinction between the reorder level and the amount to be ordered. The reorder level is the number of goods left in stock that triggers a reorder. The amount to be ordered is then sent to the suppliers.

Check your understanding

1 Describe the inputs and outputs at a POS terminal.

2 Explain the purpose of a stock control system.

3 Define

  a) stock

  b) stock level

  c) stock control

Go online for answers

Using the computer

The operating system

The set of programs that control the running of computers is called the **operating system**. The operating system has to load before any applications can be run which is why computers often take a while to **boot**.

Functions of an operating system

An operating system

- loads and runs programs
- makes the best use of the immediate access store (RAM)
- handles inputs and outputs from peripheral devices
- deals with interrupts, e.g. signals from a printer that has run out of paper
- manages the security of the system.

Microsoft Windows is an example of an operating system.

Types of operating system

- **Single program**, where only one program at a time can run.
- **Batch processing**, where data is collected in a **batch** over a period of time and then processed at off-peak times, such as nights or weekends, with minimum human intervention.
- **Multi-programming**, where more than one program is running and the computer gives each one a small amount of processing time in turn.
- **Multi-access**, where many workstations have access to one central processing unit.

- **Distributed system**, where the processing and resources are shared between a number of different computers.
- **Process control system**, where sensors monitor a process and a dedicated computer processes and acts on the data it receives.
- **Parallel processing**, where large tasks are shared between several processors in parallel.

Interfaces

The **Human–Computer Interface** (**HCI**) is the boundary where the user and the computer meet. It is usually just called the **user interface**. There are several types of user interface.

Command line interface (CLI)

The user types in a command at a prompt character.

Advantages	Disadvantages
<ul><li>The instructions are executed quickly.</li><li>A large number of options are available for each instruction.</li><li>They use less memory than other operating systems.</li></ul>	<ul><li>You need to learn the special instructions used.</li><li>Mistyping an instruction can stop the execution of the command.</li><li>Some commands and their options are very complex.</li></ul>

Graphical User Interface (GUI)

Small pictures called icons are displayed on a screen called a **desktop**. These represent programs or **shortcuts**. An icon is selected using a pointer guided by a mouse. GUIs use **WIMP** (Windows, Icons, Menus, Pointers) environments.

Exam tip

An **office assistant** will automatically sense the type of task you are carrying out. If, for example, you are trying to write a letter, then the office assistant will recognise this and prompt you with the appropriate layout for a letter.

Advantages	Disadvantages
● Low-level ICT skills are needed. ● A GUI is an easy-to-use intuitive interface. ● Pictures are more easily understood than words. ● Help is available through office assistants. ● Online tutorials are available if connected to the internet. ● Desktops can be customised.	● It can use up a lot of a computer's resources. ● It may run slowly.

Speech interface

Some user interfaces accept spoken commands using a microphone.

Advantages	Disadvantages
● Useful if the user is unable to use their hands. ● A user can issue commands while their hands are busy, such as a pilot flying a fighter plane.	● People speak using different tones, accents, pitch and distinctness which makes it difficult for the computer to interpret. ● People speak different languages and the interface may not understand them all.

Menus and dialogue boxes

Revised

A list of options is displayed using a menu.

Exam tip

Some menu options point to other menus known as sub-menus.

Advantages	Disadvantages
● Easy to navigate. ● Nothing to learn because all options are displayed in the menu. ● Validates input by limiting entries to the options shown.	● Some options may not mean anything to the user. ● It is sometimes difficult to find options if there are too many menus and sub-menus.

Touch-sensitive applications

Revised

In a **touch-sensitive device**, the position where the device is touched is sensed and used as input data.

Advantages	Disadvantages
● Low-level ICT skills are needed. ● No moving parts, so little possibility of damage. ● Easier to keep clean. ● Can be used in dirty environments or where pushing keys might be difficult (e.g. while wearing protective gloves).	● May become dirty and difficult to read. ● May be difficult to read because of reflections/glare from light.

Biometrics

Revised

Biometric systems use physical characteristics to identify a user. Inputs might be from

- ● a fingerprint
- ● the retina (eye) scan
- ● the voice
- ● facial features.

Advantages	Disadvantages
● No key needed. ● No password to forget. ● Extremely difficult to pretend to be someone else.	● Possibility of mistaken identity because of human error in recording the original data. ● Some people may not possess the physical characteristic being measured.

Check your understanding

Tested

1 Name **three** different types of operating system.

2 Explain the advantages and disadvantages of using a GUI.

3 Explain why a retina scan would not always work.

Go online for answers

Online

Banking and ICT

Bank cheques

When you need to make a payment using this method, you fill in (write) a **cheque** and give it to the person being paid. They will then give it to their bank for processing. There are five items that need to be filled in

- the date
- the name of the person (or business) being paid
- the amount in words
- the amount in figures
- a signature.

Magnetic ink character recognition

Magnetic Ink Character Recognition (**MICR**) is the process which reads particular data from cheques and inputs it to a computer.

There are three items of data encoded using Magnetic Ink Characters, at the bottom of every cheque.

- The cheque number. Each cheque in the book has a different number.
- The customer's account number.
- The branch sort code. Every branch of each bank has a unique number to identify it.

The bank prints a fourth number after it has received the cheque, which is the amount of money.

> **Exam tip**
>
> The number of cheques received at all banks every day get sent to a **central clearing house** to be sorted.

Cheques	
Advantages	**Disadvantages**
<ul><li>A large number of cheques can be read very quickly.</li><li>Crumpled or dirty cheques can still be read. It will make no difference to the readability of a cheque if ink or coffee is spilled all over it!</li><li>The characters are difficult to forge.</li></ul>	<ul><li>The equipment is expensive. MICR systems need special readers and also printers that use the magnetic ink.</li><li>Only a very limited number of characters can be used.</li></ul>

Automatic teller machine

An **automatic teller machine** (**ATM**) is a device that allows customers to

- withdraw cash from their account
- print a balance (the amount of money left in their account)
- print a small statement – this will show details of the last few transactions that have been made
- order a new cheque book
- change their Personal Identification Number (PIN).

> **Exam tip**
>
> Banking generally uses a **real-time system**, so customers cannot withdraw money from one ATM and then rush down the road and draw the same money again from another.

Home banking

Home banking is when people manage their financial affairs from home using the telephone or a website. Almost the only thing not possible is withdrawing cash.

Home banking allows you to

- view a statement of an account
- transfer money from one account to another
- pay bills
- set up or alter standing orders or direct debits
- apply for loans or mortgages.

Banks need dependable security measures and some of these measures include

- encrypting data
- computer programs monitoring customer spending habits
- not accepting direct emails from customers.

E-commerce systems

E-commerce is buying and selling using the internet.

Advantages	Disadvantages
<ul><li>The range of goods available is very large.</li><li>Shopping can be done from home, avoiding the need for the time and expense of travelling to the shops.</li><li>No need to travel home with large or heavy goods as they can be delivered directly to your home.</li><li>A business operating an e-commerce website does not have to pay for premises such as an office or a shop.</li><li>Businesses can easily expand their market to anywhere in the world.</li></ul>	<ul><li>There can be a long wait before an item arrives.</li><li>You cannot touch or smell the goods you are buying.</li><li>If the business or the customer does not take sensible precautions credit card details might be used by unscrupulous people.</li></ul>

Payroll

Employees are usually paid at the end of every week or month. The wages paid to the employees is known as the **payroll**.

Input

The sources of data used as input may include

- a database of employees' details, such as employee identity number, name, pay rate or salary, National Insurance number and tax code
- the number of hours an employee has worked during the time period
- any overtime or days off taken.

The computer will need to calculate

- the gross amount that each employee has earned
- any bonuses or overtime earned
- deductions, such as National Insurance, tax or pension scheme payments
- the net amount that each employee needs to be paid.

Output

- Printed payslips
- Messages to the bank so that money can be transferred to the employee's bank account.
- Various reports summarising the money paid out.

A payroll system is an example of a **batch processing system**.

- Timesheets and files are prepared and collected over a fixed period.
- The payroll is run at an off-peak time such as at night or at the weekend.
- There is no human intervention required once the process has started.
- The payslips are prepared and printed automatically.

Mail handling methods

- Post is collected from boxes and post offices.
- Parcels and letters are sent to a central sorting office.
- Parcels are separated from letters.
- Letters are placed in a sorting machine that reads the **postcode**.

- Letters are sorted automatically into postcode areas.
- Letters with a postcode starting CF, for instance, will be sent to the Cardiff sorting office.
- Here they are sorted by machine into batches of CF1, CF2 etc. and sent out for delivery.

Check your understanding

1. Give an example of a transaction that uses
   a) batch processing
   b) real-time processing.
2. a) What is an ATM?
   b) Describe some activities you can carry out using an ATM.
3. a) What is MICR?
   b) Explain the advantages and disadvantages of using MICR.

Go online for answers

Process control

Process control in industry

Revised

Process control is an example of a **real-time** system. Data received from sensors by the controlling computer is immediately analysed using a stored program, and this allows the system to respond immediately to any variations in the processing.

The output from the system will change the data the sensors are reading so this new data is processed which in turn will change the outputs again. This cycle is endlessly repeated and is called a **feedback system**.

Process control	
Advantages	**Disadvantages**
● Little human interaction is needed. ● The process can continue 24 hours a day, every day. ● Automatic and immediate response to problems. ● Safety for workers is improved.	● Expensive equipment and computer hardware needs to be purchased and installed. ● It has created some unemployment. ● Some problems may arise which need human decisions.

Robotics

Revised

A robot is a machine that can be programmed to perform a sequence of actions. Robots are able to carry out

● repetitive, boring jobs perfectly every time

● dangerous jobs that might harm humans, such as working in very hot or very cold areas

● precision jobs where a machine can be more accurate than a human, such as cutting steel precisely

● heavy jobs where humans could not manage the weights to be lifted.

Among many other things, industrial robots can

● assemble parts

● weld or rivet

● spray paint

● lift and carry parts (robots can follow tracks on the floor and fetch parts from a warehouse)

● handle machine tools, such as drills or grinders

● turn objects, such as tightening bolts to a specified tightness.

Robots can be programmed in two ways.

● Instructions can be written using a special computer programming language.

● Robots are guided through the actions manually and the robot will remember the movements.

> **Exam tip**
>
> Robots work as a feedback system. They have sensors to input data, a control program to analyse the signals and send messages to the actuators that cause the robot to carry out its actions.

Bionics

Revised

Bionics is the attempt to link machines to living things, such as giving a person an artificial limb that can be controlled by the human brain. Scientists are trying to advance medical treatment by creating more and more lifelike parts of the human body to help prolong life and to help people recover from accidents and disease.

Artificial intelligence

Revised

Artificial Intelligence (AI) gives systems or machines the appearance of being intelligent.

Predictive text on mobile phones is an example of AI. Other examples are

- chess playing machines
- systems that can read handwriting or understand speech
- systems that can recognise objects or even a human face
- systems that examine the way people walk and deduce their intentions, for example, alerting security when a possible car thief is detected in a car park.

Expert systems

Revised

An **expert system** is a system that takes the place of a human expert.

A database of knowledge can be searched and deductions made on the basis of the search results.

An expert system simulates the knowledge and skill of an expert.

- It has a large database of knowledge which can be interrogated.
- It has an inference engine that allows the computer to make deductions based on the facts that have been input and the data in the knowledge database.

Expert systems	
Advantages	**Disadvantages**
• The knowledge in the database can be far more than a human is capable of remembering. • An expert system should never get facts wrong. • An expert system lives: it may evolve and improve over time. • Some people would prefer to enter personal data into a computer than discuss it with a doctor.	• Some people may prefer the personal touch rather than dealing with a machine. • Expert systems are not cheap and considerable expenditure is needed to install one.

Autonomous vehicles

Revised

An autonomous vehicle, sometimes known as a driverless car, uses a variety of techniques such as radar, GPS and sensors to detect its position and to note obstacles such as other traffic and traffic lights. An on-board computer interprets all the inputs and controls the speed and direction of the car.

Check your understanding

Tested

You may be asked to discuss any of these process control systems, so you should be prepared to

- describe the system
- explain the inputs and outputs
- give the advantages of the system
- give the disadvantages of the system.

Go online for answers

Online

ICT and employment

ICT in the home and workplace

ICT has changed the way we work and enjoy our leisure in many ways.

Some jobs have disappeared as they have become unnecessary or have been replaced by computers and automated machinery.

The types of jobs that have been lost are

- boring, repetitive jobs in factories that are now carried out by robotic machines
- jobs in hostile environments – for example, robots now spray paint cars in a car assembly plant
- typists and filing clerks who have been replaced by computer filing systems
- automatic stock control replaces shop workers counting goods
- online shopping has caused some small shops to close
- fewer people work in banks because automated systems like ATMs perform many of the tasks of traditional bank staff.

However a large number of jobs have been created because of ICT

- Computer programmers
- Systems analysts
- ICT technicians
- Hardware designers
- Website designers
- Database managers

Retraining

ICT has changed the way we work, making life at work easier and ensuring maximum productivity, but the introduction of ICT has caused some job losses and created many new jobs.

The jobs that have been created need different types of skills and therefore people have to be **retrained** so

- they can carry out these new jobs effectively
- they can use new equipment or new software
- to make sure that their ICT skills are up to date
- businesses can remain competitive and productive.

Training can be done using

- websites
- interactive CDs that allow staff to learn at their own pace, in their own time and at home if they wish
- computer-assisted learning (CAL) software, which makes sure the staff learn exactly the right skills to be able to carry out their work.

Changes in working practices

ICT has caused many changes in the way that work is carried out, particularly in the way that people communicate with each other.

- Mobile phones are being used more often because they can be carried around and used anywhere. People can be contacted on the mobile phone at any time so they do not have to be in the office.

- Email is used to send messages. There is less need to write a letter and post it in a letter box. If copies of a document need to be sent to another office, then they can be sent using a fax machine.
- The hours that people can work are extending because, for example, a laptop can be taken home or used on the train commuting to or from work to catch up on unfinished tasks.
- Buying or ordering goods and materials can be done online over the internet instead of sending an order through the post or having to visit a shop or warehouse.

Teleworking

Revised

Many people are working from home and using ICT methods to communicate with their place of business or clients. This is called teleworking, and involves the use of email, the internet and fax machines.

Exam tip

Teleworking is sometimes called telecommuting or home-working.

Teleworking	
Advantages	**Disadvantages**
<ul><li>No travel expenses.</li><li>No time wasted in travelling to work.</li><li>Flexible hours – the teleworker has greater choice of when and how long to work.</li><li>Employers do not have to provide office space or facilities, such as a canteen.</li></ul>	<ul><li>There is less social interaction and teleworkers may feel isolated.</li><li>There may be more distractions in the home environment (e.g. children, domestic jobs, callers, etc.).</li><li>It may be more difficult for the management to check on whether work is being properly carried out.</li></ul>

Video conferencing

Revised

Teleconferences, sometimes called **video conferences**, are held using computers linked to the internet, and the participants can communicate with each other using

- microphones to communicate the voice
- speakers to hear the other participants
- cameras to record visual images
- screens to see each other
- special video conferencing software installed on all computers used.

Video conferencing	
Advantages	**Disadvantages**
<ul><li>It is not necessary for people to travel to the meeting so time is saved.</li><li>People can attend the meeting from their home or their office.</li><li>There is no need for expenses such as buying travel tickets or hotel accommodation.</li><li>Meetings can be called at short notice as no one needs to travel.</li><li>It does not matter where in the world the participants are so long as they have access to a video conferencing computer.</li></ul>	<ul><li>People prefer to meet face-to-face with others when important decisions need to be made.</li><li>Meetings held on computers lack the personal touch.</li><li>The video conferencing equipment needs to be bought. Microphones, speakers and video cameras are required on each of the computers and the necessary software installed. This can be expensive.</li><li>The sound and pictures may not be completely synchronised and may appear a little 'jerky'.</li></ul>

Check your understanding

Tested

1 Name **three** jobs created by ICT.
2 List the advantages of video conferencing
3 Explain the advantages and disadvantages of working from home.

Go online for answers

Online

The effects of using ICT

Economic impact of ICT

Businesses are now able to offer their goods and services to people overseas through websites. These can be viewed by anybody in any country in the world, provided they have a computer or smart phone with internet access. People can also buy goods from companies overseas by ordering them through a website.

This globalisation of business has

● expanded markets

● allowed companies to streamline their operations so they can employ fewer people

● decreased their expenses

● maximised profits.

If people buy goods through a website, a company

● no longer needs to buy/rent and equip shops

● no longer needs to employ managers and assistants to run shops

● has reduced utility bills and property taxes

● can ship goods directly from a warehouse to the customer's doorstep.

It can be argued that rich countries are gaining at the expense of poorer countries whose shares of the global market are extremely small. However, mobile telephones and wiser use of computers is helping poorer communities and in some countries driving revolution for change.

The environmental impact of ICT

The environmental impact on ICT is greater than we think. We must be careful about the use of ICT and the effect of this use on the environment. The following can reduce the environmental impact of ICT.

● Use recycled paper or store documents on a hard drive rather than using paper and so save the forest resources.

● Manage the life cycle of ICT equipment carefully by upgrading where possible rather than replacing the entire piece. Manufacturing of ICT equipment uses natural resources and generates carbon emissions.

● Dispose of old equipment carefully. Hardware contains a number of harmful elements. If the equipment is dumped in landfill harmful chemicals can eventually get into the water supply or contaminate growing things.

● Reduce the amount of energy consumed by switching off the computer or peripheral devices when not in use. Set up energy saving schemes on the computer.

● ICT equipment tends to generate heat, but why not open a window rather than switch on air-conditioning?

● Businesses should consider using video conferencing rather than sending delegates to meetings. This reduces the carbon footprint of these meetings by cutting down on travelling.

More people are working from home, saving on expenditure of fuel and time, but the home still has to be heated and ICT equipment used. There is a balance between the energy saved by not heating and lighting offices and saving on travelling, and having every worker heating and lighting their homes all day and having more time for leisure travel and shopping.

Social impact of ICT

Revised

ICT is making it easier to monitor what people are doing.

- CCTV cameras are everywhere in towns and cities.
- Communications from phone calls, emails and text messaging can be monitored.
- Satellites with cameras are capable of seeing what you are reading or identify a car number plate.
- Google® Earth lets anyone see anywhere on earth or even travel virtually the streets of unfamiliar towns.
- We can be tracked by mobile phone signals or our use of debit and credit cards.
- We voluntarily leave our thoughts and pictures on Facebook, YouTube, Twitter and blogs.
- Most governments are creating databases of DNA.
- Many governments have introduced identity cards and biometric passports.

It is important that laws are passed to protect the individual from these threats to their privacy and a balance needs to be taken between what is beneficial (e.g. cutting down crime) and harmful (invasion of privacy).

ICT helps to form political opinion with survey groups, such as YouGov, allowing politicians and businesses to constantly monitor how people are thinking and to change the way they govern accordingly.

The internet allows the public to share experiences all over the world. This has meant that different groups can air their views to the world, and radio and TV broadcasts, especially news, can be seen and heard anywhere in the world.

In 2011, it became possible to fill in the census online, and it may be that in the future voting in the UK will be done from home using the internet.

Check your understanding

Tested

1 Describe some of the jobs created by using ICT in the workplace.
2 Discuss the social changes brought about by ICT in our everyday lives.
3 Discuss the advantages and disadvantages of video conferencing.

Go online for answers

Online

Responsibilities

General Data Protection Regulation (GDPR) — Revised

This EU law is part of the British Data Protection Act (2018). The GDPR deals with data held about an individual. This is known as **personal data** and is defined as any data that could identify an individual in any way. There are many organisations and businesses that hold our personal data, such as

- the Tax Office
- a doctor or a dentist
- the Driver and Vehicle Licensing Agency (DVLA)
- any online shopping, gaming or social media site to which you sign up
- the police.

The GDPR refers to the **data subject**, the data controller and the **data processor**.

- The data subject is the individual whose personal data is stored on a computer.
- The data controller is the person in an organisation who decides the purpose of collecting the data and how it will be used.
- The data processor is the person in an organisation who processes the data on behalf of the data controller.

In smaller organisations, the data controller and the data processor may be the same person.

The GDPR defines some data as '**Sensitive Personal Data**' that must not be disclosed or processed without the data subject's knowledge and consent. Sensitive Personal Data includes data about the subject's

- racial or ethnic origin
- religious or philosophical beliefs
- political opinions
- trade union membership
- health
- genetic or biometric data
- sex life or sexual orientation.

There are some exceptions to the regulation. These include collection of data for

- national security
- detection of crime
- scientific or historical research
- processing wages, pensions or tax
- data used privately at home for household or recreational reasons.

Computer Misuse Act (1990) — Revised

The Computer Misuse Act (1990) is a law that makes it illegal to

- gain unauthorised access to files stored on a computer system, including viewing and copying the files
- gain unauthorised access to files and use them for criminal activities such as fraud or blackmail
- change or delete any files unless authorised to do so – this includes creating or planting viruses.

Electronic Communications Act (2000) — Revised

The Act was passed

- to set up a register of cryptographers
- to help e-commerce
- to recognise digital signatures as legal.

> **Exam tip**
>
> A cryptographer helps to encrypt data so that it is meaningless unless you have a key to decode it.

Regulation of Investigatory Powers Act (2000)

Revised

This Act makes it illegal to intercept emails, phone calls, letters and other communications without permission. This helps protect the individual from the state and means that groups, such as the police, cannot eavesdrop on conversations without special permission.

The Health and Safety at Work Act (1974)

Revised

Health and safety issues are discussed on pages 49–50.

The Act makes provision

- for securing the health, safety and welfare of people at work
- to protect others against risks to health or safety in connection with the activities of people at work
- to control the keeping and use of dangerous substances
- to control certain emissions into the atmosphere.

Freedom of Information Act (2000)

Revised

This Act provides public access to information held by public authorities such as government departments, local authorities and the NHS.

- Authorities must publish certain information about their activities.
- This includes printed documents, computer files, letters, emails, photographs and sound or video recordings.
- Members of the public are entitled to request information from public authorities.

Computer crime

Revised

A number of crimes are associated with the widespread use of computers.

Identity theft

Phishing is when an email pretends to come from an official organisation, such as a bank, asking you to send personal details, such as passwords and your bank account number. The purpose is to steal your identity and empty your bank account.

To prevent identity theft

- never give out bank details or passwords on emails
- do not throw away receipts, bills or statements without tearing them up or shredding them first
- check your bank and credit card statements regularly
- make sure nobody watches you when you enter a PIN at an ATM
- do not write down passwords
- change passwords regularly.

Computer viruses

Guard against computer viruses by

- only using reputable websites
- installing and using virus protection software
- never downloading illegal copies of software
- updating your anti-virus software regularly.

Check your understanding

Tested

1 Describe the rights of an individual given by the Data Protection Act.
2 Explain why it is necessary to have a Health and Safety Act.
3 Describe what is meant by sensitive personal data.

Go online for answers

Online

Safety of data and units used in computing

Data protection methods

Data and files stored on computers must be protected from damage or deletion whether accidental or malicious. Networked computers are particularly vulnerable so security has to be taken seriously.

Threats may include

- hackers
- viruses
- hardware breakdown
- human error.

Actions that can help to secure data include the following.

- Every authorised user should use a username and a password. This should reduce the chance of hacking. (Hacking is the unauthorised access to data with the intent of altering, deleting or copying the data without permission.)
- Use biometric scans of physical characteristics to restrict access to the data.
- Use different levels of security, for example where the manager can access all areas of the system but the secretary can access a much more limited area (for example, not the payroll files). This is sometimes called a hierarchy of passwords.
- Set the access rights of a file. This means that only certain people are allowed to access the data in that file. A user may have
  - no rights to access a file at all
  - the right to view but not change a file
  - full control so the file can be viewed and altered.
- Encrypt the data so that it will be meaningless to someone who does not possess the decryption key.
- Use a transaction log (which is a history of the actions that have occurred over a period of time) to monitor who has logged in, when they did and what they did while logged in.
- A firewall should help prevent hackers from gaining access to the data.
- Install and use up-to-date antivirus software.
- Backup data regularly and store the backup copy off site in a secure location.

Units used in ICT

In the system of counting you use every day, you use something called the decimal (or base 10) system.

The binary system is used in ICT. This is sometimes called the base 2 number system because there are only two digits in it. These are 0 and 1, and all data held in the memory of a computer is made up of combinations of 0s and 1s.

Counting in base 2

Decimal	0	1	2	3	4	5	6	7	8	9	10	15	20
Binary	0	1	10	11	100	101	110	111	1000	1001	1010	1111	10100

The following table shows the units we use to measure storage in a computer or any device connected to computers.

Unit	Description
1 bit is a 0 or a 1.	It can be used to represent two-state things such as TRUE or FALSE, MALE or FEMALE, YES or NO.
1 byte is 8 bits.	A byte can hold a character, such as the letter A or the character 7 or the symbol ?.
1 kilobyte (1 kB) is 1024 bytes.	A kilobyte can hold 1024 characters.
1 megabyte (1 MB) is 1024 kB.	A megabyte is about the size of a digital photo.
1 gigabyte (GB) is 1024 MB.	A gigabyte can hold approximately one billion characters.
1 terabyte (TB) is 1024 GB.	External hard drives are often able to hold a terabyte (approximately one trillion bytes) or more of data.

The hexadecimal (base 16) system is used in computing because it is easy to convert binary numbers into hexadecimal numbers and they are much easier to write down and say than long binary numbers.

Counting in hexadecimal

Decimal	0	1	2	3	4	5	6	7	8	9	10	15	20
Hexadecimal	0	1	2	3	4	5	6	7	8	9	A	F	14

When we describe the colour white, for example, using the RGB system it could be represented

- in decimal as 255, 255, 255
- in binary as 11111111, 11111111, 11111111
- in hexadecimal as FF, FF, FF.

> **Exam tip**
>
> The colour white is made by using all of the elements of red, green and blue, whereas the colour black uses none of them.

Check your understanding

Tested

1 List possible threats to data security.

2 Describe a transaction log and what it is used for.

3 Copy and complete the table below.

Decimal	Binary	Hexadecimal
1		
	101	
		A
		12
32		
255	11111111	

Go online for answers

Online

My notes

My notes

My notes